# On Comfort

D1042073

# OTHER BOOKS BY THE AUTHOR

# J. Vernon McGee

# On Comfort

## Words of Hope for the Hurting

**THOMAS NELSON PUBLISHERS**
Nashville • Atlanta • London • Vancouver

© 1994 by Thru the Bible Radio

All rights reserved. Written permission must be secured from the publisher to use or reproduce any part of this book, except for brief quotations in critical reviews or articles.

Published in Nashville, Tennessee, by Thomas Nelson, Inc.

Scripture quotations are from the KING JAMES VERSION of the Bible; the AMERICAN STANDARD VERSION; and the *New Scofield Reference Bible*, © 1967, Oxford University Press, Inc., New York, used by permission.

### Library of Congress Cataloging-in-Publication Data

McGee, J. Vernon (John Vernon), 1904–1988
    On comfort: words of hope for the hurting / J. Vernon McGee.
      p.    cm.
    ISBN 0-7852-8199-1
    1. Consolation—Sermons.  2. Sermons, American.  3. Suffering—
Religious aspects—Christianity—Sermons.  I. Title.
BV4905.2.M314   1994
252.'.56—dc20                                     93-50162
                                                               CIP

Printed in the United States of America
3 4 5 6 7 — 98 97

# On Comfort

# Contents

# THE GOD OF ALL COMFORT

This message of comfort opens on a very high level and an exalted plane of praise:

**Blessed be God, even the Father of our Lord Jesus Christ, the Father of mercies, and the God of all comfort.** (2 Corinthians 1:3)

The word *blessed* means "praise," and it has to do with worship and adoration of God. And will you notice that the apostle Paul always draws us to the praise and adoration and worship of our God. Actually, this verse is a doxology. You have in this one verse the Book of Psalms, all congealed and condensed and brought together. It is "Blessed be God [praise God] even the Father of our Lord Jesus Christ, the Father of mercies, and the God of all comfort." This is about the same as saying, "Praise God from whom all mercies flow," and I think that would be better than the word *blessings* used in the Doxology we sing on Sunday mornings. It is the same, of course, "Praise God from whom all *mercies* flow."

Now Paul mentions in this verse two of these wonderful mercies specifically. He says first of all that God is "the Father of mercies," and I like that. Whatever the mercy might be, God is the Father of it. I don't care what it is, everything that you and I have—and are—is a mercy from God. And this means that goodness and mercy are never earned. You never work for it. You never deserve it. If you do, then it's not goodness and mercy. It's given to those who are in need, because it's not a sugarplum of indulgence from an overindulgent parent either. It's a mercy which is something that God gives to those who need the very thing that He offers to them. He is the Father of mercy. You and I today have received mercies from God and

He's the Father of every one of them which we have received.

He also is the God of all comfort. That is the second specific, and may I say that I'm convinced this is the most stupendous claim that can be made for God. Paul makes here the exaggerated claim that God can comfort His child in any and every circumstance of life, that He can meet every need and He can quiet every heart, that He is the God of all comfort! And, my friend, that is either true or it is not true.

It does seem to be a highly exaggerated and overly extravagant claim for God. In fact, Paul seems to have adopted the vocabulary of the politician. You would think that God is a candidate for some office. And by the way, I've listened very carefully the past few days to the candidates for office, and I want to tell you, they are promising what only God can deliver. They claim to be able to solve all the problems of this troubled world and soothe the hurt of a disturbed people, and that just happens to be God's department. Unfortunately, our nation right now is listening to the politicians. There's one thing for sure, most are not listening to God. To them God seems rather unreal, certainly not as real as the politicians are. And the promises therefore that God makes—because He is way up yonder and we're way down here—seem to be theoretical and idealistic. But the politician is flesh and blood; he's quite real, and the crowd likes to reach out and touch him, shake his hand. I don't know why they want to do that, but somehow they feel like it will all come true if they can only touch him. May I say to you, the politician may be real, but his promises belong in fiction, and it's only dream stuff. They have never made them good, so why do you think they will make them good this year? It's always the same old story. Men continue to turn their backs on God because they think He's not real.

I wish that He could be as real to all of us today as He was to the little girl in the whimsical story I heard about. It was many years ago—I'm of the opinion some of you don't even recall that the trains once had upper and lower berths. It was always a problem to get in that upper berth, but I became an expert at that, by the way. Now this was a family of three who were traveling by train. The little girl in the family hadn't been on a train before. She was young and was rather frightened.

So that night the father and mother climbed into an upper berth, and they put the little girl in a lower berth. The little girl, down there by herself, began to whimper. The mother reached down to shush her and said to her, "Honey, God is with you, don't be afraid." So the little one was quiet for a few moments. Then she said, "Daddy, are you up there?" And he reached out and said, "Yes, I'm up here." And in a few minutes she said, "Mommy, are you up there?" and her Mommy reached down and said, "Yes, I'm here." A very exhausted traveling man in an upper berth across the aisle said, "Little girl, we're all here. Your mama is here, your daddy is here, your brother is here, your sister is here, your aunt is here, your uncle is here, your cousins are here, we're all here. Let's go to sleep!" So it was quiet for another few moments, but the stillness was broken by the soft voice of the little girl. She said, "Mommy, was that God?"

God was very real to her. I wish He could be that real to us in these days in which we live. We need the reality of God. He is the God of all comfort.

Let's look at that again, in verses 3 and 4.

# ON COMFORT

**Blessed be God [Praise God] even the Father of our Lord Jesus Christ, the Father of mercies, and the God of all comfort; who comforteth us in all our tribulation [trouble], that we may be able to comfort them which are in any trouble, by the comfort wherewith we ourselves are comforted of God.**

He is the God of all comfort. Paul tested this in the crucible of life, and the acid of suffering was poured on him. He found out it was true, but you and I today need to know whether it is authentic or counterfeit, whether it is genuine or fake.

He's "the God of all comfort." Now the popular notion of the meaning of the word *comfort* has in it a note of weakness and sentimentality. A great many people think comfort means that you come over and pat somebody on the arm, or pat them somewhere else, but it has to do with more than patting. It's sort of like saccharin and old lace. In fact, there is a whiskey named "Southern Comfort," and that just doesn't happen to be the proper name for whiskey any more than it should be for marijuana—and some think that is a comfort. One of the reasons people turn to drink and to dope today is to try to find this thing they call "comfort." But that's not really what they are looking for.

Second Corinthians 1:3 is the beginning of a section of five verses that is truly one of the most notable passages in the Scriptures. The theme, evidently, is comfort. That word or a cognate of it occurs ten times in five verses. It occurs four times in verse 4 itself. Therefore Paul is bearing down upon this word *comfort*.

We are looking for what the meaning of the word really is. The word that is used here in all ten of these instances comes from the verb *parakaleo*. *Kaleo* means "to call"; *para* means "to the side of." It means someone who is called to the side of another. In fact, the Holy Spirit is called "the Comforter." That is one of His names—in fact, that *is* His name. The Lord Jesus said to His own there in the Upper Room when they actually began to be disturbed because He had announced He was leaving them, "I will not leave you comfortless." The word is *orphanos*—"I will not leave you orphans. I'm coming to you." How is He coming? "I will send the Comforter," the *paraclete*—that's the word used here, someone to be at your side. And, my friend, it hasn't anything in the world to do with sentimentality. It means one who is a helper, a strengthener, an advocate, a lawyer, if you please.

G. Campbell Morgan and Samuel Chadwick, two great preachers of England in the past, were walking together and assessing this word *paraclete*. And the Rev. Chadwick said, "I think the best word for the Holy Spirit is *Comforter*, not *Advocate*, because an advocate is a lawyer, and my lawyer doesn't comfort me." But Dr. Morgan said, "I disagree with you. My knowledge of law is limited. In fact, I know nothing of law, so when a problem comes up I call my lawyer in, and he's my comforter, he's my helper." May I say, that is the meaning of it.

Let me give a personal illustration. When I was to be hospitalized for cancer surgery, added to my problems was another one. Of all times, the Internal Revenue Service decided they would like to check up on me. I guess they wanted to get me before I left. My wife could not make it clear to the lady who called that I was in no condition for that. Frankly, it disturbed me a great deal, and I called my assistant, Dr. Cole. He made several well-placed calls so that they let me off the hook for a little while. May I say to you that when Dr. Cole came out to the hospital before surgery, had prayer and shook hands with me, it was comforting. But that wasn't near the comfort it was when he helped me with the IRS when I had called on him. A comforter is one who helps you, one who comes in and helps you in your need, one who strengthens, one who relieves the loneliness in your life. A comforter comes to assuage the grief and calm the fears, to help in time of terrifying trouble. That's the meaning of comforter.

Notice how the word is used in Psalm 30:

**Hear, O Lord, and have mercy upon me: Lord, be thou my helper.** (Psalm 30:10)

That's it. That is the word comforter. That is what it means, "Lord, be thou my helper." Now this is what Paul is talking about, nothing sentimental— you can get rid of your old lace concept and all that which has to do with sentimentality. He is talking about one who helps us in time of trouble. Paul is simply stating the fact that our God is the Father of mercies, and He is the God of all comfort.

The question therefore arises: in what areas of life do we really need help? Where is that desperate need today for the human family? I'm going to mention only two, but you probably will think of other areas—there are many other areas.

## NEEDED: A DELIVERER

First of all, let me say that we need a Savior from sin, a deliverer from the guilt and power of sin. That is our greatest and most desperate need of all. Paul could say to the Romans—in summing up the section on sin in which he was not attempting to prove anything but stating that which was evident then and even more evident today—that man is a sinner, alienated from Almighty God. Actually he is in rebellion, not only against God, but he's in rebellion against himself and against all authority. Paul said at the end of that section,

**Now we know that what things soever the law saith, it saith to them who are under the law: that every mouth may be stopped, and all the world may become guilty before God.** (Romans 3:19)

You and I live in a world that's not on trial, not on trial at all. The sentence has already been handed in. Guilty. The day of execution hasn't come, but it is coming.

You and I live in a world in which it is said of each individual, "You are guilty before God." Each one of us bears that awful guilt. The mark of Cain is on every one of us, and psychologists call it the guilt complex.

A book review came out some years ago on the different approach that psychology was making in regard to guilt. The Freudian idea was to submerge or get rid of the guilt complex, that it was similar to an appendix—you could cut the thing off and so be rid of it. But this subsequent approach is to recognize it and to acknowledge that you do have a guilt complex—every individual has it. It operates in many different ways in our lives, but we all have it.

A leading psychologist who taught at the University of Southern California attended our Thursday Night Bible study for several years. One night as he was leaving, after making some cursory remarks about the subject he said to me, "McGee, you could have made it a lot stronger." He said, holding up his arm, "The guilt complex that you and I have is as real as that arm is. And psychology can no more get rid of that guilt complex than it can get rid of that arm." The whole world is guilty before God today, my beloved. People differ as to the way of trying to remove it, but the human family today is subject to a higher power, and we must give an account.

In the Book of Proverbs the writer asks this rhetorical question in 20:9: "Who can say, I have made my heart clean, I am pure from my sin?" In other words, God says you can't get rid of that awareness of guilt, and neither can the psychiatrist get rid of it for you. He can move it to another area, but he cannot get rid of it.

And again in Proverbs 30:12, "There is a generation that are pure in their own eyes, and yet is not washed from their filthiness." May I say to you, we may build up some sort of system whereby we say we are not guilty, but it does not disturb the reality that down underneath this awful thing is festering. And behind it is the thought that we must give an account of ourselves. Mankind is to be judged, and the Word of God closes on the note that everyone who has turned his back on Jesus Christ will have to come before the Great White Throne for judgment. The books are to be opened, and everyone must give an account of himself there to God.

My friend, how can I be delivered from that guilt? How can I escape the One on the throne saying to me, "You are guilty, you are a sinner and you are lost"? The Judge on the throne has already handed down the verdict. He says I am guilty and I need help. I need a public defender. This is the thing Job had in mind when that poor man cried out in his desperation,

**O that one might plead for a man with God, as a man pleadeth for his neighbour!** (Job 16:21)

And again he said,

**If I justify myself, mine own mouth shall condemn me: if I say, I am perfect, it shall also prove me perverse.** (Job 9:20)

Then he went on—

**For he [God] is not a man, as I am, that I should answer him, and we should come together in judgment. Neither is there any daysman betwixt us, that might lay his hand upon us both.** (Job 9:32, 33)

In other words, Job says, "In my problem that I have, if there was only someone who could take hold of the hand of God and take hold of my hand and somehow bring us together. I need help!"

Well, since the days of Job the help has come. I cry out for help and there is One at my side today. He died on the cross about 2000 years ago, a vicarious, substitutionary death. He was delivered for my offenses, He was raised for my justification, that I might stand before God. And I want to say to you today, my case has already been tried, I have already been executed. And I already stand in the person of Christ. I need a helper, I have a helper. He's the Savior.

Years ago, down in Alabama, this story was told: A very famous judge had a wayward son. His boy got involved in crime. The boy was arrested and, according to the normal course of the court, the boy's trial would come before the father. The regular thing and probably the ethical thing would have been for the judge to step aside and let someone else try the case. But folk were amazed when the father who was the judge said, "I intend to try the boy." Well, everyone was tremendously interested now because they felt, "This means the boy will get off!" The trial proceeded and finally it was time for the judge to render the decision. He called the boy up to stand in the prisoner's box. As the boy stood there, the court absolutely was thunderstruck when the judge said to the boy, "You are guilty, and you will have to pay to the full extent of the law for your crime." The boy was shocked too. Then this father who was the judge got up from the bench and he started to walk around toward his son. As he did so, he said, "Also the law says that another can come forward and volunteer to pay the penalty." And he came down to where the boy was standing and said, "Move over, son," and the boy moved over. Then the judge looked up at the empty bench and said, "I accept the penalty." And he *paid* it.

Let me be personal again. When God looked down and said to Vernon McGee, "You are guilty," I thank God I had a Helper. He took my place. He paid the penalty. He is my Comforter. He is my Helper.

## NEEDED: ASSURANCE

Now let's consider the second desperate need of the human family. We need assurance of the presence of God in all the circumstances of life. This, I would say, is an area of great need right now. We need Someone to come into the loneliness that engulfs us during that desperate darkness of life. Friends can only touch you. Christianity today is only a theory to many people. To many professing Christians and church members it is a garment that they put on for Sunday or special occasions. They wear it lightly. It's a stagnant ritual or it is an empty vocabulary.

Someone reported to me that some time ago a group of preachers in Southern California attended a convention at Church of the Open Door where I preached. They came into the auditorium and one of the preachers, as guide for the group, pointed up at the pulpit and said, "Gentlemen, this pulpit has been the greatest pulpit in Southern California on Sunday morning for fifty years." Now I want to disagree with that. It is not true, and I'm prepared to say that I don't think it has ever been true.

Do you know where the greatest pulpit is in Southern California? It's not in operation only on Sunday morning. Rather, it's Monday morning in the home, in the office, in the workshop, in the schoolroom. It's out yonder in the shopping center. It's in suburbia. It's down here where the stockbrokers walk. That's the pulpit. My friend, if what is said from this pulpit on a Sunday morning cannot be geared into work clothes and walk in shoe leather, it's nonsense, perfect nonsense.

Listen again to what Paul is saying, "Who comforts us in all our troubles that we may be able to comfort them who are in any trouble, by the comfort with which we ourselves are comforted of God." This thing was not a theory with Paul and, may I say to you, he very frankly gives us his personal experience. Listen to him,

> For we would not, brethren, have you ignorant of our trouble which came to us in Asia [Asia Minor], that we were pressed out of measure, above strength, insomuch that we despaired even of life: but we had the sentence of death in ourselves, that we should not trust in ourselves, but in God which raiseth the dead: who delivered us from so great a death, and doth deliver: in whom we trust that he will yet deliver us. (2 Corinthians 1:8–10)

Now Paul was sick, nigh unto death. The fact of the matter is, he said he had the sentence of death in him. The doctor told him he would die. Paul was the same flesh and blood that we are, and he was praying. Paul is speaking out of experience, and I'm not sure to what experience Paul is referring. Further on in this epistle we read that he was stoned yonder in the city of Lystra, left for dead. But I don't think he's referring to that here. I think he is referring to something which apparently is not recorded in the Book of Acts. He took sick, and it looked as if he would die. As Paul looked into the future, he saw nothing, and he was afraid. That's normal. But his hope was in God. He says here, "But we had the sentence of death in ourselves, that we should not trust in ourselves, but in God which raiseth the dead." He found himself cast right into the arms of God. And God let him see that beyond death there is the resurrection, and that brought hope to him.

That is wonderful, but we need to add something to it. A dear lady in the Indianapolis area sent me a card while I was recovering from cancer surgery, and she was very profuse in expressing her sympathy. She wrote, "Sometime in eternity, Dr. McGee, you and I will stand and look out into the vast space, and then we will look into the face of the Savior." She meant well, but I want to tell you very candidly, that was not very comforting. I believe that, certainly, but brother, I'm not ready to look into those vast spaces of eternity! I'd like to look around here a little longer.

Paul was very pragmatic too, and notice what God did for him, and this is very precious to me:

**Who delivered us from so great a death, and doth deliver: in whom we trust that he will yet deliver us.** (2 Corinthians 1:10)

Paul says, "He has delivered me. I've been up against death before." When he came over the wall in a basket yonder in Damascus, he was face to face with death. When he was arrested in Jerusalem, he was face to face with death. This man said he was in deaths often. He also said, "He hath delivered me." And then he said, "He does deliver me right now." Paul says, "I can have confidence in Him because He delivers me right now. He is my helper. He's the God of all comfort."

Now pay close attention to what Paul writes because this man is an apostle who had the gift of an apostle—which no one has today: ". . . and I trust he will yet deliver me." There is no arrogant and proud boasting here. He's walking softly. He said, "He comforted me. He has delivered me. He is delivering me right now. And I trust that He's going to deliver me in the future." That's the way God comforts.

Will you notice now what he says on the basis of this:

**Ye also helping together by prayer for us, that for the gift bestowed upon us by the means of many persons thanks may be given by many on our behalf.** (2 Corinthians 1:11)

Paul said, "I'm appealing to the church for prayer in this dark hour." And in that day the church responded, and God heard the prayer, and Paul was delivered. The church could glorify God, and no man got the glory. Isn't that wonderful?

My dear friend, you and I have scriptural ground for asking for prayer. Paul asks for prayer because he says, "God has delivered me, He does deliver me," and he adds, "I don't know that He will, but I trust He will deliver me in the future." That makes you walk very close to Him. It makes you look to Him in a new way.

## ALL FOR OTHERS

In conclusion we must come back to verse 4,

**Who comforteth us in all our tribulation [trouble], that we may be able to comfort them which are in any trouble, by the comfort wherewith we ourselves are comforted of God.**

This is the whole nub of the matter. It is the great principle of the Christian faith to comfort them who are in any trouble. Everything today that you and I are and that we have is for the benefit of others. God never gave you, as a child of His, anything for your selfish use. He gave it to you to share with others. I don't care what it is, you are to share it with others for His glory.

As you may know, Paul could ask the most embarrassing questions. Oh, in these past few months of teaching through the Bible I've learned a great many new things about God and about His servants. Paul had a way of probing in and asking the most personal and humbling questions. Here is just one of them:

**For who maketh thee to differ from another? and what hast thou that thou didst not receive? now**

**if thou didst receive it, why dost thou glory, as if thou hadst not received it?** (1 Corinthians 4:7)

What is it you have that you did not receive? I begin to feel around in my pockets, and I say, "Well, brother Paul, I don't have anything that I didn't receive." My friend, everything you or I have today, we received it. Do you have health? He gave that to you, whether you believe it or not. Do you have a certain amount of this world's goods? Could you be called wealthy? Do you think He made you wealthy for your sake? He did not. You are to share it with others. Has He given you youth today? He has given you youth so that you might share it with others.

I was thrilled with a letter I received from a young fellow which contradicts the theory that you have to put the old senior citizen in one place and the youth in another place. This boy worked during the summer with a man who is retired, and he wrote: "You know, I didn't like it at first, being put with this old man, but he started me at noon listening to your program when we'd sit down and eat our lunch. I'd like you to know that as a result I'm entering the ministry, and I'm starting to school this fall." May I say to you that if you have youth today it's a gift of God. "Remember now thy Creator in the days of thy youth . . ." (Ecclesiastes 12:1). You have a talent. Do you think God gave you that talent for your exploitation, so that you can use it for your own glory? Do you think God has given you a gift today for you to use for yourself? He did not.

Our Lord even gives you suffering that you might share the comfort you receive from Him with somebody who is suffering! The most comforting letter I received while recovering from surgery was from a woman up in Yakima, Washington, dying of cancer. I want to tell you, she comforted me.

Many others sent words of comfort and verses of Scripture, but this one coming from another individual who was going through deep waters meant a great deal to me:

**He shall not be afraid of evil tidings: his heart is fixed, trusting in the Lord. His heart is established, he shall not be afraid. . . . (Psalm 112:7, 8)**

She had suffered, and she comforted me.

# I Needed the Quiet

*I needed the quiet, so He drew me
   aside*
*Into the shadows where we could
   confide,*
*Away from the bustle where all the day
   long*
*I hurried and worried when active and
   strong.*

*I needed the quiet, though at first I
   rebelled.*
*But gently, so gently, my cross He
   upheld*
*And whispered so sweetly of spiritual
   things.*
*Though weakened in body, my spirit
   took wings*
*To heights never dreamed of when
   active and gay.*
*He loved me so greatly, He drew me
   away.*
                    —Alice Hansche Mortenson

# — 2 —

# CHANGING BITTER
# WATERS TO SWEET

So Moses brought Israel from the Red Sea, and
they went out into the wilderness of Shur; and
they went three days in the wilderness, and found
no water. And when they came to Marah, they
could not drink of the waters of Marah, for they
were bitter; therefore the name of it was called
Marah. And the people murmured against Moses,
saying, What shall we drink? And he cried unto
the LORD; and the LORD showed him a tree, which
when he had cast into the waters, the waters were
made sweet. . . . (Exodus 15:22-25)

This remarkable experience of the people of Israel is our subject, but to get into the water I want to use a springboard, and it's over in the letter which the apostle Paul sent to Christians in Corinth. It is this statement:

**Now all these things happened unto them for examples, and they are written for our admonition, upon whom the ends of the ages are come.** (1 Corinthians 10:11)

After reciting how God provided both food and drink for Israel during their long trek through the wilderness, Paul makes a surprising declaration. He says that their experiences were recorded for us! Why? They are examples for you and me as we walk the pilgrim pathway through the wilderness of this world. And then he gives us an admonition in the next verse:

**Wherefore, let him that thinketh he standeth take heed lest he fall.** (1 Corinthians 10:12)

Now what the children of Israel experienced while going through the wilderness corresponds to our Christian experience. You can translate what happened to them over to the lives of believers today. We can expect to encounter the same problems and expect the same solutions to work for us. Every believer is going to experience his own particular version of what happened to these people in the wilderness.

Recorded here are seven definite experiences that the people of Israel encountered as they journeyed from the Red Sea to Mount Sinai. In this message we will look at three of them. And these are common experiences of Christians, experiences that are shared by all of us.

Now I do not believe that *any* child of God can escape going through any of these experiences. They come normally and naturally into our lives. Therefore it will be profitable for you and me to follow the children of Israel for just a little way into the wilderness. I think we shall learn something by so doing.

When they crossed the Red Sea, they crossed as a redeemed people. I would emphasize that, because something we need to understand is that God had redeemed them by blood and by power out of the land of Egypt. And when they had crossed over the Red Sea and come safely to the other side, they sang the song of Moses. Up to that point they murmured and complained—they actually wanted to go back into Egypt, back to the brickyards. But then God marvelously and miraculously opened the Red Sea—due to the faith of Moses—and they crossed over.

Then these people believed, they entered the wilderness by faith, and they could sing the song of Moses. Let me lift out only a couple of verses to show that they were a redeemed people and understood this fact.

> **The LORD is my strength and song, and he is become my salvation; he is my God, and I will prepare him an habitation; my father's God, and I will exalt him.** (Exodus 15:2)

Having crossed the Red Sea, they could say: "God is my salvation." They were a saved people, if you please.

> **Thou in thy mercy hast led forth the people whom thou hast redeemed; thou hast guided them in thy strength unto thy holy habitation.** (Exodus 15:13)

They are calling themselves a redeemed people, saved and redeemed. They have crossed the Red Sea and are singing as a redeemed people.

It's interesting that as you go through the Word

of God you will find that only redeemed people sing—I mean sing praise to God with joy, and sing from the heart. Anybody can sing the blues, but to sing from the heart with joy you must be a redeemed person. So they began their march through the wilderness with a song and great joy.

How inexpressibly wonderful this was! All their lives they had been slaves in the land of Egypt, without a ray of hope on the horizon that they would ever be free. They were born into the brickyards of Egypt, and they would stay there until death. There was no hope, not a flicker of hope.

Then something wonderful happened! Moses appeared back in the land of Egypt and said, "God has sent me." And through the plagues of judgment upon Egypt, God brought these people out, redeeming them by blood on that night of the Passover and by power at the Red Sea when they crossed over.

Imagine . . . now this tremendous company of people start through the wilderness, and they don't have to go back into the brickyards to make brick. No longer will they feel the lash of the taskmaster. No longer will they groan under the burdens of Egypt. They are free! And they sing a song of redemption. Read all of their song in Exodus 15. It's wonderful!

But then they were confronted with their first wilderness experience.

## NO WATER

**So Moses brought Israel from the Red Sea, and they went out into the wilderness of Shur; and they went three days in the wilderness, and found no water.** (Exodus 15:22)

Now that's bad, isn't it? Here is a redeemed people and they start out through the wilderness according to God's instruction. They go three days without finding water. And they are crossing an arid and bleak wasteland, a desert that's as dry as anything in Arizona or California. It's *bad*, if you please.

Moses came to know that wilderness well. After living in it for forty years keeping sheep for his father-in-law, he spent another forty years there with the people of Israel! Eighty years in a wilderness puts a man in the position of being an authority, and near the end of those years this is the way

Moses labeled the place in the Book of Deuteronomy: "that great and *terrible* wilderness" (1:19). And again in 32:10, "the waste, howling wilderness"! That's what it was. Lack of water was one of their biggest problems—if God had not provided for them, they would have perished.

They traveled for three days and all of their supply was exhausted. I'm sure that most of the families had a little jug or a little canteen filled with water which they had brought out with them from the land of Egypt. But it's all gone now. And oh, they have a vehement craving for something to drink. They're parched, they're desperate—three days and no water.

## BUT WHY?

Now, my beloved, their experience is contrary to the accepted notion which people have even today of how life should be for the child of God. Here is the way it would have happened if you were reading a fairy tale: Every thorn on every cactus in that wilderness would be taken off. Every sharp stone would be removed from their pathway. The mountains would be smoothed out and the valleys would be filled in, and God's chosen people would go through the wilderness with no problems, no difficulties, no hardships—not a care, not a burden, not a sigh nor a tear.

Isn't that the way we hear some people present the Christian life today? According to them, if you have become a Christian you have solved all your problems and all your difficulties, and from here on, brother, it's easy sailing.

But the moment the children of Israel were redeemed and got on the other side of the Red Sea, they were faced with bigger problems than they ever had in the land of Egypt.

There was a certain freedom in slavery. And you know there is a certain slavery in freedom. After all, in Egypt they didn't worry about where they lived, they didn't worry about what they ate, they didn't worry about their drink, because the man who owned them took care of that.

May I say, friend, any kind of a welfare state will eventually make a slave of the individual. America is today moving rapidly toward becoming a welfare state. And a great many are not even conscious of what is really taking place right now in this land of ours. We are losing our liberties on every hand. The minute somebody else takes charge of you, that very moment you lose your liberty and you become a slave.

## NEW THIRST

Egypt was called the breadbasket of the ancient world. That was the reason the patriarch Jacob and his sons moved down there in the first place. The famine was throughout the world in their day, and they went down to Egypt because that was the only place where they could get grain.

In the land of Egypt there was water and there was grain in abundance. Egypt did not have to depend on rainfall, they depended on the river Nile—they even worshiped it! It overflowed its banks every spring and there was water in abundance. In Egypt you could fill your teakettle anytime you wanted to. But for the people of Israel out there on that torrid desert, the cisterns of Egypt are far behind them, and suddenly their source of supply is cut off. They find themselves under different circumstances. In the wilderness there is always a scarcity of water, and it's a long way from one oasis to another oasis. They have not yet found the fountain of living waters. It will take them a little while to do that.

The interesting thing is, they are having a legitimate experience. It was normal and natural—certainly there is nothing wrong with thirsting. And they are not out there in that wilderness because of some sin in their lives, and they are not out of the will of God. They are very much *in* the will of God—and yet they went three days thirsty. You explain that.

May I say to you, the Bible is a mirror for every child of God to look into. Paul said, "All these things happened unto them for examples unto us." There are a thousand other experiences that Moses could have recorded. He recorded only seven because they are examples for us. My, we ought to learn the lessons because this thirsting is the experience of every born-again child of God.

If you are a child of God, am I not now describing your experience? After you were redeemed— after that time you came to Christ and you received Him as Savior and things became different—didn't you find that the cisterns of Egypt failed to satisfy you? Isn't that what happened? Remember how, right after you were saved, you attempted to continue in the same lifestyle and it didn't work, it didn't satisfy. Wasn't that your experience?

Then there was that period of soul-thirst, a yearning and a passion for the things of God. At first you had trouble finding satisfaction—perhaps still you have not found it. Sooner or later, though, if you are a child of God you are going to find where the fountain is.

I remember that many of those who were saved years ago when Billy Graham had his first campaign here in Los Angeles went into liberal churches. One man told me, "I went to a dozen churches!" He was saved but he knew almost nothing about the Bible. And you talk about going three days in the wilderness without water, this man almost died of thirst! Then somebody, out of a clear blue sky, said, "Why don't you go down to the Church of the Open Door in Los Angeles? That preacher down there is a rank fundamentalist." But this man came anyway and stayed because he was thirsty, and he found the water of the Word here.

The apostle Paul said after he was converted, "What things were gain to me, those I counted loss for Christ . . . and I count all things but loss for the excellency of the knowledge of Christ Jesus, my Lord. . . ." Then he goes on to reveal his great longing and thirst: "That I may know him, and the power of his resurrection, and the fellowship of his sufferings . . ." (Philippians 3:7,8,10). In other words, Paul said, "When I came to Christ it revolutionized my bookkeeping system—what was loss became gain, and what was gain became loss. It turned me inside out and upside down and rightside up. Oh, that I might *know* Him." How thirsty he was to know his Lord better!

And Simon Peter, when many other of the Lord's disciples left Him and the Lord asked him if he would leave also, Simon Peter replied, "Lord, to whom shall we go? Thou hast the words of eternal life" (John 6:68).

Later Peter wrote, "As newborn babes, desire the pure milk of the word . . ." (1 Peter 2:2). Have you ever seen a little one in a crib when Mother gets the formula ready and then puts it in the bottle and holds it up? If you have ever seen perpetual motion, that is it. There's not a muscle in that little body that isn't moving: hands, feet, mouth, eyes—everything is saying, "Give it to me!"

There was a convention of doctors here in Los Angeles some time back, and one of them called me and said, "Can I have lunch with you on Thursday?" I had talked with him before; he was saved about three years earlier. He held a doctor's degree, but spiritually he was a babe. So we went down to the Biltmore Hotel, and after we sat down and ordered, he said, "I want to tell you my experience." My, was he thirsty! Believe me, friend, he knew what it was to go three days in the wilderness without water.

Our Lord spoke to the woman of Samaria about this matter:

> **Jesus answered, and said unto her, Whosoever drinketh of this water shall thirst again; but whosoever drinketh of the water that I shall give him shall never thirst, but the water that I shall give him shall be in him a well of water springing up into everlasting life. The woman saith unto him, Sir, give me this water. . . .** (John 4:13–15)

She was thirsty.

Our Lord stood on that great day of the feast in

the temple and said, "If any man thirst, let him come unto me, and drink" (John 7:37).

My beloved, the great joy of our Thursday Night Bible Study was the fact that we had so many people there who were thirsty—the new converts. I enjoyed teaching them. The old saints—well, they had been filled up and nothing was running out, I guess. But the new ones, they were so thirsty! A couple told me one night, "We drive fifty miles every Thursday night, and we can hardly wait from one Thursday night to another." A lot of folk, though, had no trouble waiting. Our Lord said, "Blessed are they who do hunger and thirst after righteousness; for they shall be filled" (Matthew 5:6). I believe that thirsting is the experience of every new believer who goes three days in the wilderness without water.

And, my friend, it might be well to go back to the Red Sea to determine if you really crossed it, to see whether you are redeemed. If you are God's child, you can't go through the wilderness of this world without water and not get thirsty.

This is the first lesson we are to learn from Israel's wilderness experience.

## BITTER WATER

I come now to the second experience. Note it very carefully:

**And when they came to Marah, they could not drink of the waters of Marah, for they were bitter; therefore the name of it was called Marah.** (Exodus 15:23)

*Marah* means "bitter." If you have read the story of the Manley party that first came into California's Death Valley, you will remember how frightened they were when they got down into that valley and found only bitter water which they could not drink. They immediately sent scouts out of that valley to try to find good water.

When the people of Israel come to Marah (there are more than two million of them at this time) the water is bitter and they cannot drink it. Remember—oh, keep remembering—that they are redeemed people. They are on the line of march. God had marked their route on the map, and they are following it. They are not out of the will of God. They are at Marah because God sent them to Marah.

And will you listen to me very carefully: Bitter

experiences come to the child of God after conversion. I do not know how to explain it, but I know it happens. It is puzzling and perplexing. How many times have you heard this from a new convert, "Why does God let this happen to me?"

The apostle Peter, who knew something about suffering, said,

> **Beloved, think it not strange concerning the fiery trial which is to test you, as though some strange thing happened unto you.** (1 Peter 4:12)

He didn't write as if something was *going* to happen; he wrote it in the present tense. He said that it *is* happening to you new converts. You *are* having trouble. Trials *do* come to a new convert.

Now I can't explain it, but I can give this word of comfort: God is not punishing you, and you don't need to ask, "Why does God let this happen to me?" God is educating you, God is preparing you for something. In the pathway of every believer there is a Marah. Have you come to yours yet? If you haven't, it's out there ahead of you. Many of you have been there. Some of you are there right now.

But I have good news for you—Marah is merely

a camping ground. It isn't suburbia, it isn't a place to live—it's merely a camping ground. God brings you to Marah, but He won't leave you at Marah. But let me say again, He will bring you there. In the pathway of every believer there is marah, bitterness.

While at my first pastorate in Nashville, Tennessee, I was holding meetings in a little place I'm sure you've never heard of named Woodbury. It's in the hills of middle Tennessee, and it's a county seat.

There was an elder in that church, a doctor. I learned to love that man. He and I hunted squirrels together many times.

One night after I had spoken on the passage where our Lord sends the disciples out into a storm, he said to me, "I'll come over tonight and talk with you." And so he came over after he had made a house call.

The manse was an old-time house built before the Civil War and had a great, big fireplace. That evening we sat together around a brisk fire. The pastor was there with his wife, and the doctor came in and sat down with us.

He said, "You know, I went away to college to

study to go as a medical missionary. And when I finished medicine, I went before the board. They examined me, and they said, 'You cannot go. Your health will not permit you to go to a foreign field.'" He said, "Why, I had prepared all my life to go as a missionary, and now I am told I can't go! Honestly, in bitterness I came way up here to this little town."

I asked him, "Is the bitterness over?"

"Oh, yes," he said. "I got over it years ago."

"Do you think God was in that experience?"

"Oh, yes, I know that now."

That doctor had taken twelve young men in that town, led them to the Lord and sent them away to college. A half dozen of them had become medical doctors, and the other six had trained and were on the field as missionaries.

And I learned that the little town of Woodbury sort of rested on that doctor's shoulders. I never walked down the street with him but what somebody didn't stop to ask him something—not just about their health, but about everything! If they were going to sell a cow or a pig, they would ask his opinion!

May I say to you, how bitter it was for that young doctor to be told that he couldn't go as a medical missionary. God brought him down by Marah, but He didn't leave him there. He led him down there so He could really use him. And He did use him.

When I heard of his death years later, I wondered how Woodbury, Tennessee, got along without him. I'm sure they survived, but they missed him. My, how important he was in that little town.

God brings His own down by Marah, if you please.

I'll tell you another experience I had in my own ministry, which has been quite limited. At the church in Nashville, when I was there, the superintendent of the junior department was a maiden lady. She had premature gray hair, and I mean it was genuine. You can't tell today. It's gotten so that if a woman has gray hair it means she's young. If she's a blonde or brunette or redhead—well, you don't know if that's her natural color or not. But in that day gray hair really meant something.

She was one of the most wonderful people I ever met. Very few of the juniors she taught went to the mission field, but they all went out into life to live for God. She followed them closely and she had an influence.

She was a beautiful woman, and I asked the superintendent of the Sunday school, "Why in the world didn't Miss Anna May get married?" He told me her story: "Before World War I, there was a young man here in this church, a fine-looking young man. They started going together and they got engaged. Then the war started and he was put in uniform. We all went down to the train station to see him off. I never shall forget how tenderly he told her good-bye. But he didn't come back. He was killed in the battle of the Marne and he's buried over there. She took his picture down, put away every remembrance of him and said, 'I will never marry.' And she didn't."

There aren't many girls like that today, fellows, I'll tell you. Oh, she was the real article. Later when the superintendent and the pastor went over to see her and asked her to take charge of the children in the junior department, she said, "I've been praying that God would give me something to do. I'll take it. It will be my life's work."

God always brings His own down to the bitter

waters of Marah so that He can use them later on. And, oh, how useful she was! Hundreds of boys and girls were influenced by her.

When I first came to Los Angeles, I met a lawyer who told me, "Preacher, when I was first converted, I got my eye on a preacher and he disappointed me. I became bitter and cynical. I almost turned my back on God. How bitter I got!" Then he said, "I found out that you can't put your confidence in mere humans, Christian or not." This lawyer learned a very important lesson: You don't look to man, you look to God. Keep your eyes on Christ.

Oh, the frustration! Oh, the keen disappointment and the bitter experiences that come to God's children! And there are times when the world tumbles in on us and we wonder what to do next.

Maybe you have a little grave out on the hillside that is your Marah. Or maybe back yonder in your life you had some other experience that embittered you. God have mercy on you if you are still hanging around Marah. God never intends His children to stay there.

The question is: What do you do with your

Marahs? How do you meet them? Notice what the children of Israel did first. "And the people murmured against Moses, saying, What shall we drink?"

Oh, how many times when an experience becomes bitter have you and I said, "Lord, why? Why do You let this happen to me? Why do these bitter waters have to be in my life?"

Notice what Moses did:

> **And he cried unto the LORD; and the LORD showed him a tree, which when he had cast into the waters, the waters were made sweet: there he made for them a statute and an ordinance, and there he tested them.** (Exodus 15:25)

Is there a natural explanation for this? Well, I've heard the formula for such a chemical reaction. I sat in the class of a wonderful scholar who said that actually there is a tree that grows out there in that Sinai Peninsula which when put in bitter water will make it sweet. You can have that for what it's worth. I can give you the formula, but it's not worth that to me, because I believe this was a miracle. That tree turned the bitter waters into sweet, if you please. What is that tree for us today? That tree is the cross of Christ.

**Christ hath redeemed us from the curse of the law, being made a curse for us; for it is written, Cursed is everyone that hangeth on a tree.** (Galatians 3:13)

And He went to the tree. Oh, my friend, He was falsely accused, He was lied about, He was blasphemed, He was shamefully treated. He bore every bit of it, and He bore the curse of sin—yours and mine, if you please. It wasn't His at all. On that tree He tasted death for every person of the human family.

Do you remember the record in John 18 that tells us about the armed mob that came to Gethsemane to arrest the Lord? Simon Peter was so zealous for his Lord that he wanted to protect Him the best he could. He drew his sword and he tried to use it.

**Then said Jesus unto Peter, Put up thy sword into the sheath; the cup which my Father hath given me, shall I not drink it?** (John 18:11)

Bitter! Oh, it was bitter. And every time I drink from the cup at communion I try to concentrate on the sweetness. As I taste that sweetness I think of the cup He drank. His was a bitter cup—that cup belonged to me. He took *my* cup, the bitter cup, that I might have the *sweet* cup. He did that for me.

And, Paul can write to you and me today, "O death, where is thy sting? O grave, where is thy victory?" (1 Corinthians 15:55). Our Lord went to the cross, and He removed the bitterness, if you please. He bore the curse. Will you listen to Simon Peter again, because you and I are going to have difficulties unless we put the cross of Christ into the bitter experiences of life.

**Beloved, think it not strange concerning the fiery trial which is to try you** [or which is testing or trying you] **as though some strange thing happened unto you, but rejoice, inasmuch as ye are partakers of Christ's sufferings, that, when his glory shall be revealed, ye may be glad also with exceeding joy.** (1 Peter 4:12, 13)

You and I, when the bitter experience comes, will be made bitter unless we bring the cross of Christ to bear in that experience.

> *Must Jesus bear the cross alone*
> *and all the world go free?*
> *No, there's a cross for everyone,*
> *and there's a cross for me.*

How we need to accept that and translate it into life when the bitter experiences come to us!

## ELIM

We come now to the third wilderness experience, and we'll make it the last for this message. There were seven of them; these are only the first three.

**And they came to Elim, where were twelve wells of water, and threescore and ten palm trees; and they encamped there by the waters.** (Exodus 15:27)

Elim means "palm trees," and at Elim they had seventy of them! And beside that, they had twelve wells of water! That was some oasis, wasn't it?

Elim suggests abundant blessing and fruitfulness. After Marah, God always brings His children to Elim—". . . Weeping may endure for a night, but joy cometh in the morning" (Psalm 30:5). You may lock Peter in the inner prison, but an angel is going to spring him before morning (see Acts 12). Paul and Silas may be beaten within an inch of their lives and put in a dungeon, but at midnight they're going to sing praises to God, and the doors of the prison will be flung open (see Acts 16).

God will take you down by Marah. But He won't leave you at Marah. There is an Elim ahead for the pilgrim today. And God's plan of usefulness goes by Marah to Elim. It always has; there's no exception.

Joseph—oh, the difficulties and the problems this poor boy had! But after his father had died, his brothers came to him with fear. They were afraid he was going to take revenge on them. He said, "Wait, you meant it for evil, but God meant it for good." His Marah was when he was sold into slavery by these jealous brothers, but there was Elim down the way. God brought Joseph to the oasis where there were, in effect, palm trees and abundance of water. (See Genesis 37—50.)

David—oh, how wonderful it was to be a carefree shepherd boy. Then one day Samuel appeared and poured the anointing oil on him. After that, David is brought into the palace of Saul. My, it looks like everything is going to be easy. Some say it ought to be easy for God's man, but should it? One day David is before the king playing his harp to soothe him. By the way, I have often wondered

how it sounded—a harp with only three strings!
Maybe David wasn't a good musician because Saul
threw his spear at him! Have you ever felt that
way about these modern musicians?

But seriously, the reason Saul tried to kill David
was because of his hatred towards him, and from
that day on David took to the wilderness and the
caves. Finally he even cried out to God, "I'm
hunted like a partridge." There's always a closed
season on birds, but there was no closed season
on David! He was being hunted constantly by Saul,
and he lived like a partridge in the mountains!

But there came a day when God placed David
on the throne. This rough and rugged man became
the king of all Israel. He's God's man, and he went
down by Marah, but God brought him to Elim.

Since America passed the log-cabin days and the
rugged frontier was pushed into the Pacific Ocean,
we have not produced a great man. We now have
millionaires for presidents—I'm not talking poli-
tics—but no millionaire could be a president of
the caliber of Abraham Lincoln. We will never
again have another president out of a log cabin.

Life today lacks that touch which produces character and greatness, that which takes a man

through a period where he eats the bread of adversity and drinks the water of affliction so that he can say as the apostle Paul said, "I know both how to be abased, and I know how to abound . . ." (Philippians 4:12).

In this affluent and comfortable society in which you and I live, we may know how to *abound*, but how many today know how to be *abased*? My beloved, how we need to be abased, yet be able to trace the rainbow through the rain, as George Matheson wrote in the beloved hymn, "O Love That Will Not Let Me Go."

> *O joy that seeketh me through pain,*
> *I cannot close my heart to Thee;*
> *I trace the rainbow through the rain,*
> *And feel the promise is not vain,*
> *That morn shall tearless be.*

You can't have that rainbow without the rain.

Has God brought you down by Marah? You thought He made a mistake, didn't you? And you thought you were out of the will of God. But He did it for a purpose, because He takes all of His children down by Marah. But, my friend, don't stay there. Don't live there in bitterness. Take the cross of Christ and put it into those bitter waters.

Have you been mistreated? Jesus was mistreated. Have you been lied about? He was lied about. Have you been unable to defend yourself? He chose not to. When He was falsely accused, He didn't open His mouth. Do you feel like there's been injustice in your life? Well, have you read the account of His trial? They nailed Him to a cross—it was the greatest crime of history! May I say, your little Marah and my little Marah are nothing compared to His. But put that cross into your experience and it will turn your bitter waters to sweet.

Then go on to Elim. There are seventy palm trees there. And twelve springs of water!

# IN MEMORY OF
# RUTH MARGARET McGEE

*She was so small, but her influence was so great; her life was short, but the memory of her is long.*

*"And Jesus called a little child unto him . . ."* (Matthew 18:2).

*"Suffer little children to come unto me, and forbid them not: for of such is the kingdom of God"* (Luke 18:16).

# — 3 —

# DEATH OF
# A LITTLE CHILD

At the death of my firstborn, God gave me some words of comfort which I desire to pass on to parents and to loved ones of little ones who die. There is no sorrow quite so heartrending as the death of a little child. The image of the little one is written so indelibly upon the mind and heart that during the long watches of the night it appears on memory's screen to haunt us. If the child lives long enough to walk and to talk, the faltering steps and childish prattle are like a lingering fragrance in the home that seems so strangely silent. The arms are empty, the eyes are filled with tears, and the heart is like a vacant house. Yet, there is no affliction for which God has provided such tender comfort and such sweet solace. He is "the God of all comfort" (2 Corinthians 1:3).

The following comforts are mentioned with the prayer that the Comforter, the Holy Spirit, will apply them to broken hearts and to wounded spirits as strong splints and sweet ointment.

## A BRIEF LIFE IS NOT AN INCOMPLETE LIFE

We sometimes feel that a life which was so brief was in vain and that God has mocked us by giving us the little one and then by taking it away immediately. The child had no opportunity to perform a work, nor was there any time given to develop character. Let us remember, first of all, that the little one had an eternal spirit and that it has gone into the presence of God where there will be an eternity to perform works and develop character.

With eternity as a measuring rod, the long life of Methuselah was merely a pinpoint on the calendar of time. Although the span of life of your little one was brief, your child completed a mission, served a purpose, and performed a God-appointed task in this world. The child's presence turned your thoughts to the best. Your little one's helplessness brought out your strength and protection, and your child's loveliness roused your tenderness and love. The little one's influence will linger in your heart as long as you live. If anything can bring a man to God, it is a child. "A little child shall lead them" is not idle rhetoric. We think of Methuselah in connection with old age, but did you ever consider him as an infant? Well, he was once a baby, and a most arresting thing is recorded about his birth. He was the son of Enoch, and it is written: "And Enoch lived sixty and five years, and begat Methuselah: *and Enoch walked with God after he begat Methuselah* three hundred years, and begat sons and daughters: and all the days of Enoch were three hundred sixty and five years: and Enoch walked with God: and he was not; for God took him" (Genesis 5:21-24). We do not know what the life of Enoch was for the first sixty-five years, but when the day came that he looked down into a crib at a little boy named Methuselah, he began to walk with God. If

Methuselah had died in his crib, he would have accomplished about as much as evidently he did in his long life.

Your little one served its purpose. A brief life is not an incomplete life.

## YOU CAN BE ASSURED THAT ALL IS WELL WITH THE CHILD

David lost two sons for whom he grieved deeply. One was Bathsheba's child, who died shortly after birth. David was greatly exercised about the life of this child. The record reveals the magnitude of his grief:

**David therefore besought God for the child; and David fasted, and went in, and lay all night upon the earth. And the elders of his house arose, and went to him, to raise him up from the earth: but he would not, neither did he eat bread with them. And it came to pass on the seventh day, that the child died. And the servants of David feared to tell him that the child was dead: for they said, Behold, while the child was yet alive, we spake unto him, and he would not hearken unto our voice: how will he then vex himself, if we tell him**

that the child is dead? But when David saw that his servants whispered, David perceived that the child was dead: therefore David said unto his servants, Is the child dead? And they said, He is dead. Then David arose from the earth, and washed, and anointed himself, and changed his apparel, and came into the house of the LORD, and worshipped: then he came to his own house; and when he required, they set bread before him, and he did eat. Then said his servants unto him, What thing is this that thou hast done? thou didst fast and weep for the child, while it was alive; but when the child was dead, thou didst rise and eat bread. And he said, While the child was yet alive, I fasted and wept: for I said, Who can tell whether GOD will be gracious to me, that the child may live? But now he is dead, wherefore should I fast? can I bring him back again? I shall go to him, but he shall not return to me. (2 Samuel 12:16–23)

David knew that the child was with the redeemed and that he would join him someday by death and would be with him forever.

David had another son, Absalom, who in manhood became rebellious and sinned grievously. While ruthlessly attempting to seize the kingdom from his father, he was killed in battle. Upon learning of his death, King David, a strong, rugged old soldier, wept as a woman. The Bible records his appalling grief:

**And the king was much moved, and went up to the chamber over the gate, and wept: and as he went, thus he said, O my son Absalom, my son, my son Absalom! would God I had died for thee, O Absalom, my son, my son!** (2 Samuel 18:33)

David did not know the destiny of the soul of Absalom, or at least he doubted his salvation. David wished it had been possible to have died in his stead so that Absalom might have another chance. David could be sure of the first child, but he was not sure of Absalom.

You, likewise, may have the assurance of the salvation of your little child; it is "safe in the arms of Jesus." You would be willing to turn over your child to the care of a faithful nurse in this life, and you can rejoice that your little one is in the arms of the Good Shepherd who is more tender than any human nurse. In fact, the little one is better off than if it were asleep in its crib in your home. It is beyond this veil of tears. There is no danger or evil to beset its pathway. We may rest in the confidence that our children are safe with Christ. Remember that when He was here on earth, He took up little ones into His arms, saying, "Suffer little children to come unto me, and forbid them not: for of such is the kingdom of God" (Luke 18:16). On another occasion He said, "Take heed that ye despise not one of these little ones; for I say unto you, that in heaven their angels do always behold the face of my Father which is in heaven" (Matthew 18:10).

If you could but know the blessedness of your little one at this very moment, it would reconcile you to the loss of the darling of your heart.

## HEAVEN SHOULD BE MORE REAL TO YOU

The Lord Jesus has gone to prepare a place for those who are His own. Part of this preparation is the taking of your child. Heaven will mean more to you now—your dearest treasure is there. And where your treasure is, there will your heart be also. He takes from the family here to form the family there. Baby hands are beckoning to you, and a baby voice is calling you home.

I did not realize how many parents there were who had lost children until our first baby was taken. One after another in the congregation came with tears in their eyes to tell of their secret sorrow. One dear lady and her husband always sat down in the front pew. They were elderly and they had a son who was a great sorrow. In spite of this, they were always smiling and seemed never to be defeated by life. I shall never forget my surprise when I discovered the reason for this as they told me of the loss of their firstborn and of their happy anticipation of seeing the little one in heaven someday.

## THERE ARE NO MISTAKES IN GOD'S PLANS

God has permitted this to happen to you. It was no accident, nor was it something over which He had no control. He knows the way you take; your times are in His hands, and He numbers the hairs of your head. Somehow and some way God will make this work out for His glory and your good.

"And we know that all things work together for good to them that love God, to them who are the called according to his purpose" (Romans 8:28). Perhaps you do not see this now, and I am sure that I cannot explain it in detail, but here is where you can trust God. He permits us to suffer here, and in this world of sin it is part of His discipline for a higher place.

> For whom the Lord loveth he chasteneth, and scourgeth every son whom he receiveth. If ye endure chastening, God dealeth with you as with sons; for what son is he whom the father chasteneth not? (Hebrews 12:6, 7)

## YOU DID THE BEST YOU COULD UNDER THE CIRCUMSTANCES

Perhaps you are rebuking yourself for not having done something more in behalf of the child. You may be harassed by a haunting fear that you did something wrong. Martha and Mary felt that the death of their brother could have been averted. They both said to Christ Jesus, "Lord, if thou hadst been here, my brother had not died" (John 11:21, 32). Yet in the providence of God it was best for

Lazarus to die, though it could have been averted—but only with divine help. Humanly speaking, you did the best you could. You are not as wise nor as strong as God. You did what you could, and you must leave the results to Him. Do not reproach yourself for negligence or ignorance. Regardless of what you had done, you are still a fallible and feeble creature. You did the best you could.

## SUPPOSE YOUR CHILD
## HAD LIVED

Multitudes of children today, growing up to maturation, are entering upon a life of crime or shame. Think of the children who bring disgrace and suffering to their parents. A father in Atlanta, Georgia, a man of wealth and who was known for his gentleness and graciousness, said to me that he wished he had buried his son the day that he sent him away to college. Think of the sad parents who have nothing but bitter memories of a debauched and godless son or daughter. Think of the anxiety of parents as their children are swept along in today's changing world. Think of the millions of starving children in many parts of the world, of the multitudes of boys and girls being brainwashed by godless ideologies. Think of the pinched faces and swollen tummies of children who are the victims of war. You will never know a haunting dread for the future of *your* child, nor will there be ever a sting in your memory.

God knew what was in the future for your child. Perhaps there would have been a life of illness, a disfiguring accident or brain damage, or a lingering, incurable disease. God knew all of this, and I am confident that He has given you the better part. You can be certain about your child's future now; you could not be certain if your little one were alive.

## YOU WILL SEE YOUR
## LITTLE ONE SOMEDAY

If you have faith in a living Savior who was victorious over death and the grave, then you will someday see your little one. We are told through the apostle Paul,

**But I would not have you to be ignorant, brethren, concerning them which are asleep, that ye sorrow**

**not, even as others which have no hope.** (1 Thessalonians 4:13)

Notice that he did not say we are not to sorrow; he said that we are not to sorrow as those who have no hope. Death is yet to be defeated. Someday the dead in Christ are to be raised from the grave,

**For the Lord himself shall descend from heaven with a shout, with the voice of the archangel, and with the trump of God: and the dead in Christ shall rise first: then we which are alive and remain shall be caught up together with them in the clouds, to meet the Lord in the air: and so shall we ever be with the Lord.** (1 Thessalonians 4:16, 17)

The little form of your child will be raised from the grave and the spirit joined to the glorified body. If you are in Christ, you at the time will be reunited, and together you will be at home with Christ forever.

Will our children be as we last saw them? I do not know nor can I prove it from Scripture (for Scripture is silent at this point), but I believe with all my heart that God will raise the little ones as such and that the mother's arms that have ached for them will have the opportunity of holding them. The father's hand that never held the little hand will be given that privilege. I believe that the little ones will grow up in heaven in the care of their earthly parents—if they are saved. One of the worst things of which I, as a father, can conceive, is of parents being in hell knowing that they cannot have their child—there are no children in hell. What an added joy this lends to heaven in looking forward to having your little one again! Though the Scriptures do not teach this explicitly, this does seem to be the sense. Remember that David expected to go to his *child*. And referring to children Christ said, "Of such is the kingdom of heaven."

## YOU CAN PROVE THE REALITY OF GOD'S COMFORT

His comfort is real; His presence is vital; His words are life. He can become a mighty reality to you now. He wants to enter into your sorrow and sympathize with you. When Jesus went to a funeral, these amazing words are recorded, "Jesus wept" (John 11:35). Because He had our humanity and was touched with the feeling of our infirmity, when He went to the cemetery, He wept—in spite of the fact that He intended to restore life.

*In every pang that rends the human heart*
*The Man of Sorrow had a part.*

There is a story of sweetness and beauty which enlightens the heart of every parent who has lost a child. It concerns a custom among the shepherd folk of the Alps. In the summertime when the grass in the lower valleys withers and dries up, the shepherds seek to lead their sheep up a winding, thorny, and stony pathway to the high grazing lands. The sheep, reluctant to take the difficult pathway infested with dangers and hardships, turn back and will not follow. The shepherds make repeated attempts, but the timid sheep will not follow. Finally a shepherd reaches into the flock and takes a little lamb and places it under his arm, then reaches in again and takes another lamb, placing it under the other arm. Then he starts up the precipitous pathway. Soon the mother sheep start to follow and afterward the entire flock. At last they ascend the torturous trail to green pastures.

The Great Shepherd of the sheep, the Lord Jesus Christ, our Savior, has reached into the flock and He has picked up your lamb. He did not do it to rob you but to lead you out and upward. He has richer and greener pastures for you, and He wants you to follow.

Will you follow Him?

You will, if you catch a glimpse

*Of the good Shepherd on the height.*
*Or climbing up the starry way,*
*Holding your little lamb asleep.*
*While like the murmur of the sea*
*Soundeth that voice along the deep*
*Saying, "Arise, and follow Me."*

# —4—

# THE DARK SIDE OF LOVE

*The little Book of Zephaniah will never take the place of the Gospel of John as number one in Bible popularity. The contents of this book have never been familiar, and I doubt that it has been read very much. I dare say that few have ever heard a sermon on Zephaniah.*

*Such neglect is not due to mediocrity or the inferiority of this little book. If its theme were known, I think it would be very much appreciated, because it has the same theme as the Gospel of John.*

*John is called the apostle of love, and as we study this book we will find that Zephaniah is the prophet of love. That may be difficult for you to believe, but let* me give you a verse to demonstrate my point. You are acquainted with John 3:16, but you may not be acquainted with Zephaniah 3:17: "The LORD, thy God, in the midst of thee is mighty; he will save, he will rejoice over thee with joy; he will rest in his love, he will joy over thee with singing." This is lovely, is it not? However, the prophecy of Zephaniah is a little different from the Gospel of John, for this verse is just a small island which is sheltered in the midst of a storm-tossed sea.

Most of this book seems rather harsh and cruel; it seems as if it is fury poured out. Chapter 3 opens in this vein: "Woe to her that is filthy and polluted, to the oppressing city!" Zephaniah's prophecy is one of judgment involving more than the land of Israel. It is a worldwide devastation that is predicted here. The Book of Revelation confirms this and places the time of this judgment as the Great Tribulation period.

During that period, this earth will absolutely be denuded by the judgments that will come upon it. This will occur right before God brings in the millennial kingdom and renews the earth.

Since there is so much judgment in this little book, how can love be its theme? To find proof that love is its theme is like looking for the proverbial needle in a haystack, but I will illustrate my point by telling you a mystery story. This may seem to be a very peculiar way *to begin a study of Zephaniah, but it is going to help us understand this little book. The title of my story is* **The Dark Side of Love.**

There is a theme about which every believer should have a clear understanding if he is to walk in full assurance. It is the *dark side of love*—God's love. And in order to make this clear, perhaps I should brief you on a terrifying scene.

It was late at night in a suburban area of one of our great cities in America. A child lay restless in her bed. A man with a very severe and stern look stealthily entered her bedroom and softly approached her bed. The moment the little girl saw him a terrified look came over her face, and she began to scream. Her mother rushed into the room and went over to her. And the trembling child threw her arms about her.

The man withdrew to the telephone, called someone who was evidently an accomplice, and in a very soft voice made some sort of arrangement. Hastily the man re-entered the room, tore the child from the mother's arms, and rushed out to a waiting car. The child was sobbing, and he attempted to stifle her cries. He drove madly down street after street until he finally pulled up before a large, sinister and foreboding-looking building. All was quiet, the building was partially dark, but there was one room upstairs ablaze with light.

The child was hurriedly taken inside, up to the lighted room, and put into the hands of the man with whom the conversation had been held over the telephone. In turn, the child was handed over to another accomplice—this time a woman—and these two took her into an inner room. The man who had brought her was left outside in the hallway. Inside the room the man plunged a gleaming, sharp knife into the vitals of that little child, and she lay as if she were dead.

Your reaction at this point may be, "I certainly hope they will catch the criminal who abducted the little girl and is responsible for such an awful crime."

However, I have not described to you the depraved and degraded action of a debased mind. I have not taken a chapter out of the life of the man in cell 2455, death row. I have not related to you the sordid and sadistic crime of a psychopathic criminal. On the contrary, I have described to you a tender act of love. In fact, I can think of no more sincere demonstration of love.

You see, that little girl had awakened in the night with severe abdominal pain. She had been subject to such attacks. It was her father who had rushed into the room. He had talked to the specialist about it, and when he saw the suffering of the little girl, he went to the telephone, called the family physician, and arranged to meet him at the hospital. He had rushed his little girl down to the hospital and had handed her over to the family physician. The doctor had taken her to the operating room and performed emergency surgery. Through it all, every move and every act of that father was of tender love, anxious care, and wise decision. I have described to you the dark side of love—but *love*, nevertheless.

The father loved the child just as much on that dark night when he took her to the hospital and delivered her to the surgeon's knife as he did the next week when he brought her flowers and candy. It was just as much a demonstration of deep affection when he delivered her into the hands of the surgeon as it was the next week when he brought her home and delivered her into the arms of her mother. My friend, love places the eternal security and permanent welfare of the object of love above any transitory or temporary comfort or present pleasure down here upon this earth. Love seeks the best interests of the beloved.

## SICKENING RATHER THAN STIMULATING

In our nation we have come through a period when the love of God has been exaggerated out of all proportion to the other attributes of our God. And it has been presented in such a way that the love of God is a weakness rather than a strength. It has been presented on the sunny side of the street with nothing of the other side ever mentioned. There is a "love" of God presented that sounds to me like the doting of grandparents rather than the vital and vigorous concern of a parent for the best interests of the child.

The liberal preacher has chanted like a parrot. He has used shopworn clichés. He has taken tired adjectives, and he has said, "God is love, God is love, God is love," until he has made it saccharine sweet, and he has not told about the dark side of the love of God. He has watered love down, making it sickening rather than stimulating, causing it to slop over on every side like a sentimental feeling rather than an abiding concern for the object of love.

## HE DEALS WITH US SEVERELY

However, I want you to notice that there is the dark side of the love of God. The Great Physician will put His child on the operating table. He will use the surgeon's knife when He sees a tumor of transgression or a deadly virus sapping our spiritual lives or when He sees the cancerous growth of sin. He does not hesitate to deal with us severely. We must learn this fact early: He loves us just as much when He is subjecting us to surgery as when He sends us candy and flowers and brings us into the sunshine.

And sometimes the Great Physician will operate without giving us so much as a sedative. But you can always be sure of one thing: When He does this, He will pour in the balm of Gilead. When He sees that it is best for you and for me to go down through the valley of suffering, that it will be for our eternal welfare, He will not hesitate to let us go down through that dark valley. Someone has expressed it in these lines:

*Is there no other way, O God,*
*Except through sorrow, pain and loss,*
*To stamp Christ's likeness on my soul,*
*No other way except the cross?*

*And then a voice stills all my soul,*
*As stilled the waves of Galilee.*
*Can'st thou not bear the furnace,*
*If midst the flames I walk with thee?*

*I bore the cross, I know its weight;*
*I drank the cup I hold for thee.*
*Can'st thou not follow where I lead?*
*I'll give thee strength, lean hard on Me!*

My friend, He loves us most when He is operating on us, "for whom the Lord loveth he chasteneth . . ." (Hebrews 12:6).

Under another figure the Lord Jesus presented it yonder in the Upper Room to those who were His own. He said in John 15:1, 2:

**I am the true vine, and my Father is the vine-dresser. Every branch in me that beareth not fruit**

**he taketh away; and every branch that beareth fruit, he purgeth [prunes] it, that it may bring forth more fruit.**

We must remember that the Father reaches into your life and mine and prunes out that which is not fruitbearing—and it hurts! But, as some Puritan divine said years ago, "The husbandman is never so close to the branch as when he is trimming it." The Father is never closer to you, my friend, than when He is reaching in and taking out of your heart and life those things that offend.

It was Spurgeon who noticed a weather vane that a farmer had on his barn. It was an unusual weather vane, for on it the farmer had the words, GOD IS LOVE. Mr. Spurgeon asked him, "Do you mean by this that God's love is as changeable as the wind?" The farmer shook his head. "No," he said, "I do not mean that God's love changes like that. I mean that whichever way the wind blows, *God is love.*"

Today it may be the soft wind from the south that He brings to blow across your life, for He loves you. And tomorrow He may let the cold blasts from the north blow over your life—and if He does, He still loves you.

It has been expressed in these familiar lines written by Annie Johnson Flint in a way I never could express it:

> *God hath not promised skies always blue,*
> *Flower-strewn pathways all our lives*
> *    through;*
> *God hath not promised sun without rain,*
> *Joy without sorrow, peace without pain.*
>
> *God hath not promised we shall not know*
> *Toil and temptation, trouble and woe;*
> *He hath not told us we shall not bear*
> *Many a burden, many a care.*
>
> *God hath not promised smooth roads and*
> *    wide,*
> *Swift, easy travel, needing no guide;*
> *Never a mountain, rocky and steep,*
> *Never a river, turbid and deep.*
>
> *But God hath promised strength for the*
> *    day,*
> *Rest for the laborer, light for the way,*
> *Grace for the trials, help from above,*
> *Unfailing sympathy, undying love.*

Beloved, if you are a child of God and are in a place of suffering, be assured and know that God loves you, regardless of how it may appear.

## GOD'S LOVE IN ZEPHANIAH

Now the little prophecy of Zephaniah sets forth the dark side of the love of God. I have a notion that very few people have ever heard a sermon on Zephaniah, and since it presents the dark side of God's love, I can well understand how it would be unpopular.

It opens with rumblings of judgment—the judgment of God that is coming upon this earth. Three verses in the first chapter are often the reason that many folk put the book down even before they get through the three short chapters. Here are verses 2, 15, and 16:

> **I will utterly consume all things from off the land, saith the LORD.**

> **That day is a day of wrath, a day of trouble and distress, a day of waste and desolation, a day of darkness and gloominess, a day of clouds and thick darkness, a day of the trumpet and alarm**

**against the fortified cities, and against the high towers.**

You see, this little book opens with a Florida hurricane, a Texas tornado, and a California earthquake.

You might get the impression, upon reading this little book, that God hates His people. You would think that He is vindictive in His judgment, that He is cruel, brutal and unfeeling as He moves forward against mankind. Perhaps the theological liberal, who a few years ago made the statement that the God of the Old Testament is a big bully, had read only the first chapter of Zephaniah. I wish he had read all of it. He would have found that the God of the Old Testament is not a big bully, but that we are shown the dark side of His love.

## GOD IS JEALOUS

And over in the third chapter of Zephaniah, verse 8, we read this:

**Therefore, wait upon me, saith the LORD, until the day that I rise up to the prey . . .**

The Great Physician is getting ready to operate.

**... for my determination is to gather the nations, that I may assemble the kingdoms, to pour upon them mine indignation, even all my fierce anger; for all the earth shall be devoured with the fire of my jealousy.**

I know that the theologian does everything he can to break down the expression "the jealousy of God" and tries to say that it really does not mean jealousy. My beloved, it does mean *jealousy!*

Sometimes you hear a wife say this, "You know, my husband is not jealous." I have news for her. He does not love her if he is not jealous—or else he is just sure that no one else would be interested in her. It is one of the two reasons, you may be sure of that.

God's Word says that He is jealous, and I cannot conceive of love that would not have that quality in it. It is not the jealousy of an Othello that is being spurred on by an Iago! This is jealousy of One who loves us and wants nothing to come into our lives that is going to hurt or harm us. He will do anything in the world to protect us.

In Zephaniah 3:2 we read:

> **She obeyed not the voice; she received not correction; she trusted not in the LORD; she drew not near to her God.**

This is the diagnosis of the Great Physician. He is saying that the nation whom He loved needed to be put on the operating table.

Even in judgment, beloved, God is love!

## GOD WILL REST IN HIS LOVE

Now notice the final section of this little book, verse 17:

> **The LORD, thy God, in the midst of thee is mighty; he will save, he will rejoice over thee with joy; he will rest in his love, he will joy over thee with singing.**

This verse is a talisman; it reaches on down into the very end of the age in which we are living. However, we are not concerned just now with the prophetic messages of Zephaniah; we want the message that is for you and me today. It is this: God wants to rejoice over you. He wants to rejoice over me. He wants to rest in His love for you and for me. This proposes a question to be faced: Can

God rejoice over you and me this day; can He rest in His love for you and for me?

In Isaiah 53:11 we read:

**He shall see of the travail of his soul, and shall be satisfied; by his knowledge shall my righteous servant justify many; for he shall bear their iniquities.**

This refers to Christ's sacrifice for the sin of the world. God is satisfied with what Christ did for the sins of this world, and if you trust in Him, you are complete in Him.

But wait just a minute! Is He satisfied with your life right now? Let me illustrate this in a very practical way.

On Mother's Day I did something that I have not done in years: I sat and listened to someone else preach. It was a wonderful sermon, and while listening I had an opportunity to do something that I do not have opportunity to do when the pressure of preaching is upon me; I sat there and looked at the folk in a very comfortable sort of way. I saw a mother wearing a lovely corsage sent to her by her son in the East. He is a prominent businessman, high up in government circles, but he is not a

Christian. She is praying for him. She has asked others to pray for him. She said to me one Sunday morning after the message, with tears streaming down her cheeks, "Oh, Dr. McGee, I pray that God will save my boy. I pray that He will save him even if He has to put him on a sick bed; even if He has to kill him—I pray that He will save him." If the FBI heard her plotting like that, would they arrest her? No, sir! She loves her boy. As I looked out last Sunday morning and saw her sitting there, the tears slipping down her cheeks, I knew this: She is not rejoicing over him with joy; she is not resting in her love. She loves him with all her heart, and if giving her life would save that boy, she would give it immediately. Although she loves him, she cannot rest in her love.

Let's go back to our question: Is God satisfied with your life right now? I do not believe God can rest in His love for you and for me until we have been brought into His likeness.

## GOD IS TRAINING HIS CHILDREN

And God knows how this can best be accomplished. Notice Hebrews 12:5, 6:

**And ye have forgotten the exhortation which speaketh unto you as unto sons, My son, despise not thou the chastening of the Lord, nor faint when thou art rebuked of him; for whom the Lord loveth he chasteneth, and scourgeth every son whom he receiveth.**

God's treatment of you today is based on the relationship that He has with you. If you are His child, He is your heavenly Father. He wants to come to the place where He can rest in His love.

There are parents today who have by work and sacrifice put away a little money in order to send their boy away to school. After the boy is in school for awhile, he writes back, "Dad, it's hard here—the assignments are too heavy and the dormitory is too strict. I'm homesick, and I want to come home!" The father writes back a stern letter, "You stay on, study hard, and apply yourself." When that boy gets the letter from his dad, he says, "I don't think my dad loves me anymore. My dad *couldn't* love me or he wouldn't want me to go through this torture."

In a similar way God is training us.

The word *chastening* in Hebrews 12:5, 6 really carries no thought of punishment at all. Rather it means *to child train*. God is training you and me, not for an earthly career, but He is preparing us for eternity. And it is His principle always to deal with His children like this.

An interesting report has come from the Palomar Observatory. I read everything that is released from Palomar, describing what they are looking at up there—I wish they would let me look, but they will not. They say that out yonder in the Milky Way in the constellation Aquarius they have discovered a doughnut-shaped constellation that is remarkable. It is unusual because in the center is a dim star. Although that dim star cannot be seen very well down here, it does not mean that it is not a hot star. Astronomers say that the temperature is 270,000 degrees Fahrenheit on that star and that it is giving off light at such a cycle that our eyes can't see the light—it is ultraviolet, it is dark light. However, the light that is being given off is "triggering" light to all of the stars round about it. God uses the dark light to bring out the bright. I do not understand that in astronomy—it is beyond my thinking—but, my friend, I see God's principle in operation there. He disciplines us in order that He might bring us out into the light.

While in college I roomed with a boy who had a great deal to say about his father who was a banker in a small Mississippi town. He was a dictator, and he ruled with an iron hand the bank, the community, every farm on which he held a mortgage, and his own household. The boy told me that when he was growing up he thought his dad was hard on him. So he used to say, after his dad had given him a sound whipping, "When I get big enough, I am going to run away from home. I'm not going to stay here under him, he's cruel and mean." The day came when he did run away from home and joined the navy. It was several years before he returned home. When he did, he said to his dad, "Dad, I want to thank you for the way you trained me. I thank you for the way you disciplined me. I thought you were mean at the time, but I thank God for it now because it has made me a better man."

My beloved, note what God says in Hebrews 12:9:

> **Furthermore, we have had fathers of our flesh who corrected us, and we gave them reverence. Shall we not much rather be in subjection unto the Father of spirits, and live?**

I hear preachers talk about the golden streets of heaven. I'll be honest with you, I don't think the golden streets of heaven are going to be the most impressive thing there. I hear people talk about the gates of pearl and, friend, although the gates of pearl will be beautiful, I do not think they will be the thrilling thing. I hear people say that God is going to wipe away all tears—that is wonderful, but that won't be the most wonderful thing of all.

## THANKS FOR TROUBLE

Rather, I think you and I are going to look back on the brief life that we lived down here and our light affliction which was but for a moment. Then we will go to God and thank Him for every burden, for every trial that He gave us down here. We are going to thank Him even for sickness—not for healing, but for sickness. And we will thank Him for every problem, every disappointment, every faithless friend, every heartache, every false accusation that ever has been made against us. I think we will go to Him and we will say, "O God, I thank Thee for putting me on the operating table and cutting out that which was hindering me." You and

I are being trained and disciplined in order that we might have a place up yonder in Glory.

Perhaps one of the finest summaries of this essential teaching is found in these beautiful lines, written by an author whose name is unknown to me. I assume it comes out of the experience of a person who had spent some time in the crucible of suffering. The title is "In the Crucible."

*Out from the mine and the darkness,*
*Out from the damp and the mold,*
*Out from the fiery furnace,*
*Cometh each grain of gold,*
*Crushed into atoms and leveled*
*Down to the humblest dust,*
*With never a heart to pity,*
*With never a hand to trust.*

*Molten and hammered and beaten,*
*Seemeth it ne'er to be done.*
*Oh! for such fiery trial,*
*What hath the poor gold done?*
*Oh! 'twere a mercy to leave it*
*Down in the damp and the mold;*
*If this is the glory of living,*
*Then better be dross than gold.*

*Under the press and the roller,*

*Into the jaws of the mint,*
*Stamped with the emblem of freedom*
*With never a flaw or a dint;*
*Oh! what a joy, the refining*
*Out of the damp and the mold!*
*And stamped with the glorious image,*
*Oh, beautiful coin of gold!*

Someday, when in the presence of our Savior, we will thank Him for every burden, every trial, and every heartache. We will thank Him for dealing with us as a wise Father deals with His children and for the dark side of His love.

# — 5 —

# WHAT DO YOU DO WITH YOUR BURDENS?

**Bear ye one another's burdens, and so fulfill the law of Christ.** (Galatians 6:2)

**For every man shall bear his own burden.** (Galatians 6:5)

Most little towns of a bygone day had a character known as the town atheist, a freethinker, generally a ne'er-do-well. The little town in which I lived as a boy lacked many things. It didn't have streetlights. In fact, we didn't have electric lights in our home, and I can remember using a kerosene lamp to study by in those days. Our little town didn't have sidewalks, it didn't have paved streets. It didn't have running water—except what you ran out to the well to get; and it didn't have inside plumbing. There were many things our little town lacked, but we did have a town atheist. He called himself a socialist. Each Sunday morning, weather permitting, he was down at the street corner on the town square, speaking. These fellows are generally loquacious, and this fellow was especially so. Usually he had about a dozen listeners who were also loafers. On my way to Sunday school—I killed as much time as possible—I always stopped to listen to him. The thing that impressed me about this atheist was that his mouth was cut on a bias, and as he chewed tobacco an amazing thing took place. He not only defied the Word of God, he also defied the law of gravitation. You would think, according to the law of gravitation, that the tobacco juice would run out of the lower corner of his mouth. But it didn't. It ran out of the upper corner. I used to stand there as a boy and wonder how he did it.

This man, I remember, always ridiculed the Bible and pointed out supposed contradictions.

His favorites were verses 2 and 5 in the sixth chapter of Galatians:

**Bear ye one another's burdens, and so fulfill the law of Christ,** and **For every man shall bear his own burden.**

He would read both verses, then lift his head, leer at the crowd and say, "You see, there is a contradiction in the Bible. One place it says that you are to bear one another's burdens, and then it says you are to bear your own burdens." None of us in the little town knew how to answer him, so we just stood there in silence and listened to him. Actually, the answer was very simple, but we didn't know it in those days.

There are in the Scriptures eleven different words that are translated by our one English word *burden*. This means there are different kinds of burdens. There are some burdens that you can share; there are other burdens that you must bear and cannot share with anyone. That is a very simple but a very satisfactory answer.

Burdens are those things that we all have in common. All of us have burdens. Not all of us have wealth, but we have burdens. Not all of us have health, but we have burdens. Not all of us have talents, but we have burdens. Some of us even lack physical members—not all of us can see, not all of us can hear, not all of us have arms and legs, and certainly not all of us have good looks. We say that we all have the same blood, but it is not the same; it comes in different types. Although we may not have very much in common, we all have burdens.

However, not all of us have the same burdens. Actually, we all have different burdens. What Paul is doing in this sixth chapter of Galatians is dividing burdens into two classes: burdens which we can share and burdens which we must bear and cannot share.

## BURDENS YOU CAN SHARE

He first refers to burdens that you can share:

**Bear ye one another's burdens, and so fulfil the law of Christ.** (Galatians 6:2)

Dr. Lenski, the Lutheran expositor, has a very fine translation of this verse: "The burdens of each other keep bearing." That is a literal translation. The Greek word for "burden" in this verse is *baros*, and it simply means "something heavy." There are other derivatives, but fundamentally and basically it simply means "something heavy." Our Lord used it when He spoke about "the *burden* and the heat of the day." And the early church, when it met in its first council in Jerusalem, made this decision: "For it seemed good to the Holy Spirit, and to us, to lay upon you no greater *burden* than these necessary things" (Acts 15:28), speaking of a burden that the Gentile churches were to share with the church in Jerusalem.

Someone has said that a load is only half a load when two are carrying it. There are burdens today that we can share.

A woman boarded a bus with a very heavy basket. She sat down beside a man and put the basket on her lap. After noticing her discomfort he said, "Lady, if you would put that heavy basket down on the floor, you would find that the bus would carry both you and your load." May I say to you, there are burdens that you can let someone else bear with you.

Again, the word *baros* can mean "fault," as we shall see. It can mean "infirmity." It can mean "tension." And it can mean "grief." These are some of its meanings.

Now what are some of the burdens that you and I can share? We will look at three of them, although there are many others.

## Faults

The first of these three is one that all of us have today. It is the burden of our faults. I think everybody has at least one fault.

A man speaking to a group asked the question, "Is there anyone here who does not have a fault, or do you know of someone who does not have a fault?" No one raised his hand. After he had repeated the question several times, a little fellow in the back, a Mr. Milquetoast type, raised his hand. The speaker asked him to stand.

"Are you the one who has no faults?"

"Oh, no," he said, "I'm not the one."

"Then do you know someone who does not have any faults?"

"Well," he said, "I don't exactly know him, but I have heard of him."

"Tell me, who is he?"

The little fellow said, "He's my wife's first husband."

And I have a notion that he had heard of him quite a few times!

All of us have faults. Notice that Paul began this sixth chapter of Galatians like this:

> **Brethren, if a man be overtaken in a fault, ye who are spiritual restore such an one in the spirit of meekness, considering thyself, lest thou also be tempted.** (Galatians 6:1)

Faults—that's a burden. And the word *fault* here means "to fall down." It is the Greek word *paraptoma*, meaning "a falling aside." Many times we fall down. Many times we see a brother fall down, and we are told, "Ye who are spiritual *restore* such an one." *Restore* is the same word used in the Greek for a physician to reset a bone. This is the meaning that is really primary here. It requires a man who is an expert, a man who has deftness and experience to reset a bone. Notice that he says, "Ye who are *spiritual* restore such an one." Oh, the clumsiness of so many people in trying to straighten out somebody else! We need to be *spiritual* to restore such an one. Also note that we are to *restore* him, not drive him out of our fellowship. The sin should be condemned—there is no toleration in the Scriptures for sin—but the sinner should be restored. Sometimes it seems as if we have gone out of the business of restoring. Instead, we are in the business of criticizing the man with the fault, the man who has fallen down.

Also notice that we are to restore "in the spirit of meekness." One of the great preachers of the South reminded me of this a few years ago when we were together. He and I had graduated from college together. We also had graduated from seminary together, and we both had worked our way through college. I worked in downtown Memphis on a newspaper, and he was the manager of a garage at night. One night I got on the streetcar to go back to the dormitory, and I saw him standing in the back of the streetcar. It was a warm night, the windows were open, and he had his head hanging out. I walked back and found that he was sick, but not only that, he was drunk. He turned to me and said, "Mac, I'm getting out of the ministry. I'm discouraged." He had been engaged to a girl in Alabama who had let him down, and he felt the whole world was against him. He said, "I'm through. I'm leaving school." I hit him on the back as hard as I dared, and said, "No, you're not." I got him off the streetcar a block before we reached the school, and I slipped him around the corner and brought him in the back door of the dorm. He didn't have a roommate at that time; so I just put him to bed with his shoes and clothes on. The next day he came to me and said, "Mac, I thank you for what you've done, but I still am going to leave." Well, I talked with him and could tell him, "I have felt just like you feel, and I could have done exactly what you did, easily." Well, he did not leave school, and I thank God for that because he is today one of the beloved preachers of the South. The Scriptures tell us:

**Brethren, if a man** [a Christian man] **be overtaken in a fault, ye who are spiritual restore such an one in the spirit of meekness, considering thyself, lest thou also be tempted.** (Galatians 6:1)

There is not a sin committed today by anyone but what you or I could have committed it. The faults of others are burdens that you and I can share.

### Tensions

Then there is another burden that you and I can share: tensions. Now you can take a tranquilizer but, my friend, that really won't solve your problems. We are living in a time of tension such as the human family has never before experienced. I don't know about you, but I live in "Tension Town." Many of us in these great metropolitan areas are under pressure and tension today. This is certainly a burden we need to bear with one another. Let me illustrate. A very dear man in one of the churches I pastored came to me and said, "Do you have something against me?"

"No," I said. "Why do you say that?"

"Well, I met you down on the street and you didn't even speak to me."

"I didn't?"

"No, you just passed me right by."

"I didn't see you."

"You must have—you looked right at me."

So I asked him what day that was and realized it was the day the airlines had gotten my tickets mixed up, and I was going down to the ticket office to straighten them out. We are under tension at a time like that. And my friend was also under tension for assuming I had snubbed him. Well, I never shall forget how he put his arm around me and said, "I'm glad to know that." You see, he was helping me bear the burden of tension. That's something we can share with each other.

## Grief

Now I come to the third burden you and I can share. That is the burden known as grief. The burden of tragedy, the burden of sorrow, the burden of disappointment are inevitable in the human family. If one hasn't come to you, it will come. And when it comes, you need a friend to stand with you. The three friends of Job are examples. We criticize them because they began a talking marathon, but actually they spent seven days sitting with Job and sorrowing with him.

In a book of natural history there is a statement that reads: "Man is the only one who at birth knows nothing and can learn nothing without being taught. He can neither speak nor walk nor eat. In short, he can do nothing at the prompting of nature but weep." All that you and I know to do when we come into this world is weep! We come into this world with a cry, and we need comfort. From the very beginning and all through life we need comfort because of the fact that we have been born into this world of woe.

Ruth could say to Boaz, "Thou hast comforted me." She was a stranger, an outcast, had come from a foreign country, and expected to be kept on the outside, but into her life came someone who showed an interest in her and extended to her certain courtesies. With appreciation she said, "Thou hast comforted me."

Mary broke open an alabaster box of very expensive perfume, and poured it upon the head of our Lord. She did this shortly before His crucifixion because she knew what was going to take place. No one else seemed to realize what was happening, but she knew. She was criticized for it, but Jesus said, "Let her alone; for the day of my burial hath she kept this" (John 12:7). She alone entered into His sufferings. And He said,

> **Verily I say unto you, Wherever this gospel shall be preached in the whole world, there shall also this, that this woman hath done, be told for a memorial of her.** (Matthew 26:13)

And the fragrance of that ointment has filled the world!

Grief is a burden that you can share. There will be those who will come to you in your sorrow.

Our faults, our tensions, our griefs—these are some of the burdens that you and I can share.

*Is thy cruse of comfort failing?*
*Rise and share it with a friend,*
*And thro' all the years of famine*
*It shall serve thee to the end.*

*Love Divine will fill thy storehouse,*
*Or thy handful still renew.*
*Scanty fare for one will often*
*Make a royal feast for two.*

*Lost and weary on the mountains,*
*Wouldst thou sleep amidst the snow?*
*Chafe that frozen form beside thee,*
*And together both shall glow.*

*Art thou wounded in life's battle?*
*Many stricken round thee moan;*
*Give to them thy precious ointment,*
*And that balm shall heal thine own.*

—Author unknown

## BURDENS YOU MUST BEAR

Now let's look at the other verse that tells us there are burdens which we cannot share.

**For every man shall bear his own burden.** (Galatians 6:5)

The word "burden" here is the Greek *phortion*, meaning a load to be borne. This word is used to speak of a ship's cargo. Actually it is used to speak of a child in the womb—only the mother could bear it, you see. This is a load that is impossible to share. While I never recommend J. B. Phillips' *The New Testament in Modern English* as a translation (it should not be called a translation), it is a most excellent explanation. Many times it throws light on a passage of Scripture. Here it gives this paraphrase of Galatians 6:5: "For every man must 'shoulder his own pack.'" That's it. Each man must shoulder his own pack. There is an old bromide: "To every man his work." And another, a rather crude one, "Every tub must sit on its own bottom." In other words, there are burdens today that you and I cannot share.

Every life in one sense is separated, it is isolated,

it is segregated, it is quarantined from every other life. Dr. Funk, of the Funk and Wagnalls Dictionary, has compiled a list of words in which the saddest word in the English language is *alone*. There are certain burdens that you and I will have to bear alone. I will mention just a few of them here, and you will think of others, I'm sure.

### Suffering

The first one I want to mention is suffering. You will have to suffer alone. No one can suffer for you. You are born alone into this world of woe, and you will suffer alone. You will have to face certain problems alone. There will be physical suffering that will come to you. You will get sick, and no one can take your place.

When my daughter was a very little thing, we were coming back to California from Texas, and she started running a high fever. We took her to the hospital at Globe, Arizona. A doctor gave her certain medication and told us, "You give her this, and the fever will go down. It is getting late in the afternoon so keep driving into California and get out of the heat." So we started out. In Phoenix we stopped for gasoline, and my wife took her temperature. It registered 104 degrees—her temperature hadn't gone down. We were frightened. We went to a motel, called a doctor, and told him the situation. He said to continue the medication and to bring her to the hospital in the morning. Never shall I forget my feelings as I carried her to the hospital and laid her down. Never in my life had I had that experience. I would have gladly taken that fever in my own body, *gladly* would I have done it. But, my friend, I could not do it. We have to suffer alone. You cannot get someone to substitute for you. Suffering is one thing that we cannot share. Mental anguish is another type of suffering that you cannot share. Oh, the number of folk who are disappointed. They are even bitter today because of some great disappointment. Suffering is a burden that we have to bear alone.

## Death

There is another burden that you and I cannot share with anyone else. It is death. There will come a time when each of us will go down through the valley of the shadow of death, and we will go alone. Thomas Hobbes, an agnostic all of his life, a very brilliant man, said when he came to his

death, "I am taking a fearful leap into the dark!"
And then he cried out, "Oh, God, it is lonely!" Yes,
it is. Death is a burden you cannot share. John
Haye, at one time Secretary of State, was quite a
writer. He wrote a poem portraying death entitled
"The Stirrup Cup," having in mind the cavalrymen
who used to drink when they mounted their
steeds.

> *My short and happy day is done*
> *The long and lonely night comes on:*
> *And at my door the pale horse stands*
> *To bear me forth to unknown lands.*

And, my friend, when death comes, you and I
will be riding alone. Death is a burden that you
will have to bear alone.

## The Bema

We come now to the last burden we will bear
alone. It has an unusual name, by the way. It is the
*Bema*. The *Bema* is the judgment seat of Christ. It
is not for the unsaved; it is for Christians. Oh yes,
there is a judgment for the unbeliever, the Great
White Throne judgment described in the twentieth
chapter of Revelation, but the *Bema* seat is for the
Christian.

**For we must all appear before the judgment seat of Christ, that everyone may receive the things done in his body, according to that he hath done, whether it be good or bad.** (2 Corinthians 5:10)

Everything that we have done in the flesh as Christians is to be judged to see whether or not we receive a reward. Salvation is not in question—that was settled for the believer at the cross of Christ. It is the works of the believer that are to be judged at the *Bema* seat.

**So, then, every one of us shall give account of himself to God.** (Romans 14:12)

Then Paul puts down a principle which is applicable to every avenue of life, but is specifically given to believers:

**Be not deceived, God is not mocked, for whatever a man soweth, that shall he also reap.** (Galatians 6:7)

This principle is true in the realm of nature. You sow cotton, you reap cotton. You sow wheat, you reap wheat. And as a Christian you will reap what you sow. We like to sing "The Old Account Was Settled Long Ago." In a believer's life this is true.

But what about the new account? What about the account since you were saved? What has your life been since you accepted Christ? Do you have sin in your life? Have you confessed it? We are all to appear before the judgment seat of Christ.

Somebody will say, "I'm a Christian. I don't have any sin." You don't? Then you are not in the light. If you will get into the light, you will see the sin that is in your life. The light, which is the Word of God, reveals what is there.

Try this one on for size: "Therefore, to him that knoweth to do good, and doeth it not, to him it is sin" (James 4:17). Does that fit you today? I think it will fit all of us. He that knows to do good, and does it not, *sins*. Your life as a child of God is a burden that you carry, and you will have to bring it before Him someday.

## A BURDEN YOU CAN NEITHER BEAR NOR SHARE

Now as I bring this message to a conclusion, I want you to see that there is another type of burden which you cannot bear nor can you share. It is a burden the Scriptures speak of: the burden of sin. Paul speaks of it in the first part of Romans. David in the Psalms says:

**For mine iniquities are gone over mine head; like an heavy burden they are too heavy for me.** (Psalm 38:4)

Sin is a burden you cannot share with anyone else. And sin is a burden you cannot bear, my friend. "My iniquities," David says, "are gone over my head; as a heavy burden they are too heavy for me." Also from the Psalms comes this longing:

**And I said, Oh, that I had wings like a dove! For then would I fly away, and be at rest.** (Psalm 55:6)

Have you ever felt like that? Sometimes the doctor recommends that we get away from it all. The psalmist said, "If I could only run away from it." But you and I cannot run away from our sin because we have a guilt complex. A psychologist out here at the University of Southern California tells me that the guilt complex is as much a part of us as our right arm. Psychologists have tried to get rid of it. They have not succeeded. Everyone has it. Sir Arthur Conan Doyle, the writer of detective stories and creator of Sherlock Holmes, liked to play practical jokes. At one time he sent a telegram to twelve famous people in London whom he knew. The telegram read, "Flee at once. All is discovered." All twelve of them left the country—yet all of them were upright citizens. May I say to you, my beloved, we all have a guilt complex. Sin is that burden which we can neither share nor bear. It is too heavy for us.

There is only one place you can get rid of it, and that is at the cross of Christ:

> **Cast thy burden upon the LORD, and he shall sustain thee; he shall never suffer the righteous to be moved.** (Psalm 55:22)

The Lord Jesus said:

> **Come unto me, all ye that labor and are heavy laden, and I will give you rest.** (Matthew 11:28)

He alone can lift the burden of sin today, and it is because He paid the penalty for it. He alone can lift it; He alone can take it from you.

There are two famous pieces of sculpture that depict this. One is the "Dying Gaul" and the other is "The Laocoön;" both are in Rome at the Vatican. "The Dying Gaul" depicts a man who has been brought as a captive and slave to Rome, put into the arena as a gladiator, and has been mortally wounded. He is lying there, his life blood flowing from him, and he is looking up for help. He is in a strange land, and there is nobody, nobody there to help him. A dying gladiator. May I say to you that this is a picture of any man today without Christ. Christ alone can help us, for that is the reason He came into the world. He said:

**For the Son of man is come to seek and to save that which was lost.** (Luke 19:10)

He also said:

**. . . The Son of man came, not to be ministered unto but to minister, and to give his life a ransom for many.** (Mark 10:45)

Christ paid the penalty for your sin and my sin. Like the dying gladiator, we can look to Him and be saved.

The other piece of sculpture is "The Laocoön." A priest of Troy looked out and saw two sea serpents come and coil themselves about his two sons. He went to their aid, but he could not help them because the sea serpents also enmeshed him in their coils. There they are—all three of them going down to death. To me this illustrates the fact that personal sin is a burden that we cannot cope with. It will take us down to death, eternal death.

What do *you* do with your burdens?

There are some burdens that you can share. There are others that you must bear alone. But the burden of personal sin is a burden too heavy for you; it is the burden you cannot bear. About 2000 years ago Christ took the burden of your sin, and He bore it on the cross. Today your burden is either on you, or by faith you have received Christ as your Savior, and it is now on Him. It cannot be in both places—your sin is either on you or it is on Christ. And Christ does not *share* it; He bore it all. Literally He said,

> **Come unto me, all ye that labor and are heavy laden, and I will rest you.** (Matthew 11:28)

# — 6 —

# WHAT DO YOU DO WITH YOUR FEARS?

## WHO IS MADE WITHOUT FEAR?

"Who is made without fear" is a relative clause in the Book of Job (41:33), but we can turn it very nicely into an interrogative clause and ask the question, "Who is made without fear?" Fears are feelings that we all share to varying and different degrees, and there are different kinds of fears. We sometimes smile at the old bromide that women are afraid of mice. But the bravest man would be mortally afraid if he knew he were going to give birth to a baby! Actually, there have been hundreds of babies born just in the first few hours of this very day, and the mothers certainly have had no band or fanfare to make the announcement that they have given birth.

Psychology lists fear, along with love and anger, as one of the strong and complex emotions of the human species. The TV, the theater, and the novels take these three emotions and mix them up like a Betty Crocker recipe. However, they don't always come out with the success that Betty Crocker seems to have with hers.

It is doubtful whether any member of the human family anywhere is devoid of fear. If he is, he's an abnormal individual. Fear is as much a part of our human makeup as eyes and nose and mouth.

The psalmist said that he belonged to the fraternity of fear, and he wrote, "I am a companion of all them that fear thee . . ." (Psalm 119:63). By the way, he said that the fraternity of fear was a secret fraternity—he said: "The secret of the LORD is with them that fear him . . ." (Psalm 25:14). David belonged to a secret fraternity of those who fear the Lord.

Fear was the first outward evidence and manifestation of the effect of the disobedience of Adam in the Garden of Eden. It was the first symptom of sin. For the very first thing that Adam did—and he confessed it—was to show fear. "And he said, I heard thy voice in the garden, and I was afraid, because I was naked . . ." (Genesis 3:10).

The first thing that this man confessed was that he was afraid. From that day, fear entered into the very web and woof of mankind. Man went out of the Garden of Eden and was told that by the sweat of his brow he would earn his bread. Driven by hunger and thirst and fear, the human family spread over this earth.

The bravest of men have feared. Moses is a man that no one could call a coward. Moses stood before Pharaoh, and the Pharaoh before whom he stood was no petty ruler. The man was a world ruler, and it took a brave man to deliver God's message to him. Also Moses stood before God yonder on Mount Sinai. It took a brave man to do that. In addition, for forty years he stood before the rebellious Israelites. It took a brave man to do that. And yet this man Moses, in the second chapter of Exodus, wrote of himself, "And Moses feared," which is the reason he left the land of Egypt at that time.

David is a man who is noted for his bravery. But if you read the Psalms, you will find that one of the emotions he mentions is fear. David, probably more often than anyone else, describes the gamut of emotions that sweep across the human soul. He plays upon the soul, as God does, as if it were a three-stringed instrument—actually one with 126 strings, for he describes the many emotions that sweep through the human heart. He was very frank when he mentioned fear. He said: "What time I am afraid, I will trust in thee" (Psalm 56:3). He admitted that he was a man of fear, yet here is a man who is known for his bravery.

Elijah was a brave man. Elijah stood before the prophets of Baal, and he stood before King Ahab. I don't know what happened to him, but I do know this: there was a great breakdown in his life when word came from Jezebel that she would have him killed. Elijah turned and *ran!* He took off for Beer-sheba, wouldn't stop there, but went as far into the desert as he could and crawled underneath a juniper tree. He does not *say* he is afraid, but his actions speak louder than any words he could give us.

May I say to you that you will find that the bravest of men have been those who have been afraid. May I also say that all of us experience something that fills our hearts with fear.

Fear, down through the history of the race, has been looked upon as a weakness of mankind. It has been looked upon as a detriment. Men have always been applauded for their bravery; they have been ridiculed for their fears. "Only cowards fear" is an accepted cliché even today, and we are ashamed of our fears.

It was Shakespeare who wrote, "Of all base passions, fear is the most accursed." Even Emerson, the Unitarian whom many delight in quoting, gives this false statement: "Fear always springs from ignorance." The most popular books following World War II were books that dealt with the subject of fear, with the general theme of freedom from fear.

My friend, the Bible has never gone along with the worldly philosophy and popular fallacy of the day. The Bible does not take the position that fear is cowardly. I have examined the many words in both the Old and New Testaments that are translated by the word "fear" and have found that they are divided into three classifications. There is the fear that is base and cowardly, craven, contemptible, and certainly to be shunned. There is another fear that is good and right and helpful, something that is a blessing to mankind. Finally, there is a third class of words that can be translated either good or evil. You have to look at the context to see whether it means good or bad.

The very interesting thing is that modern psychology has confirmed Scripture in this particular division. The fear instinct, they tell us, passes through three stages. There is a stimulating stage which is good. For example, you experience fear if you wake up at night and the house is on fire. Your pituitary gland immediately sends out an alarm to the adrenal gland, and the adrenal gland sends out into the bloodstream some extra energy so that you are able to jump and run and yell like you never did before. And after you get outside the house, you wonder how in the world you ever did it. My friend, that kind of fear is good. And the Scripture speaks of that kind of fear that leads to action, the fear that motivates you.

Then there is the second stage. It is called the arrestive or the inhibitory stage. It can be good, provided a person does not stay in that stage. He might be there for a moment, but if he stays there it is dangerous, for then he moves to the third stage which is the paralyzing stage.

Paralyzing fear is bad because it leads to all sorts of different complexes. You find people today who are afraid of germs. I knew a lady years ago who would not open a door without taking out a handkerchief to put over the doorknob; or, if she did open the door with her hand, she would go and wash her hands—not with common soap, but with soap that would destroy germs! She was off on that particular thing.

Then there are people today who are afraid of open spaces. They will not go across even a vacant lot. There are other people who are afraid of crowds. And then I do believe there is another form. I've never seen it listed—it must be common only to Southern California—and that is the fear of rain. I say this facetiously, of course.

As we've gone through the Word of God and attempted to make a careful study of the subject of fear, I believe that *fear* can be divided into two major classifications. The first fear is fear of God, and that is good. That leads to action. Also there is the fear of man, and that kind of fear, my beloved, leads to inaction. It is the kind that leads to paralysis.

It was said of Cromwell that he was the bravest man who ever lived. Someone asked Cromwell one day what was the secret of his bravery and why he was considered such a brave man. His answer was something like this: "I've learned from the Word of God that if you fear God you will not have any man to fear." May I say to you, this is the secret David learned. He wrote:

**In God have I put my trust: I will not be afraid what man can do unto me.** (Psalm 56:11)

This is so important that when you move over to the New Testament, you find this statement:

**So that we may boldly say, The Lord is my helper, and I will not fear what man shall do unto me.** (Hebrews 13:6)

My beloved, today you either have a fear of God or you have a fear of man. Either you are afraid of those things that are about you and what men say and what men do, or you are afraid of God.

Somebody will object, "I don't think we ought to be afraid of God." I believe that this is something today that needs emphasizing as it never has been emphasized before, especially in our fundamental circles where we have assumed a familiarity with God which the Scriptures will not warrant at all. Somehow or other God is regarded as only a great big brother whom we pat on the back in most familiar terms. I say to you today, friend, we do well to fear God. And if we fear Him, we will not have any man to fear.

In this message I would like to identify some common fears. I do not want to be theoretical; I want to be practical and pragmatic. And I want to limit our observations to two fears that are common today. If we fear God, we will be delivered from these fears.

## THE FEAR OF LONELINESS

The fear of being alone, when it is carried to an exaggerated degree, is a form of psychasthenia. People who are obsessed with this fear can't stand to be alone. My friend, today only God can deliver you from the fear of loneliness.

A pastor who does any counseling at all encounters many cases of marital problems in which couples are not well mated. He will often ask the question of women, very fine Christian women generally, "Why did you marry this man who is so inferior to you, who is on a much lower level than you are?" The answer women give—I've heard it again and again—is this: "Well, I was getting up in years, and I was afraid I might have to go through life alone." I want to say to you that most of them wish they *had* gone through alone because loneliness is something they should not have feared at all.

The bunco squad of the police department will tell you today that the confidence men, especially in Southern California, prey on unsuspecting folk, both men and women, who are alone and lonely.

A number of years ago a book came out by a single woman who was the editor of a popular magazine. The title of the book was *How to Live Alone and Like It*. But when you read her book, you know she was whistling in the dark and singing in the rain. She had not solved her problem at all.

Many young people are afraid to take a stand for Christ because they've reached that age where they have herd instinct, and they say, "What would the gang say? I'd lose my friends. I have the feel of the pack, and I want to be with them. If I take a stand for Christ, I will lose my friends, and I will be alone."

Likewise there are multitudes of older men and women today who could take a stand for Jesus Christ, but they are saying, "What would my friends say? What would my business associates think? What would my social cronies think of me if I took a stand for Christ?"

Let me say to you carefully that multitudes are going into a lost eternity because they are afraid of man. They ought to be afraid of God.

There's no reason to be afraid of loneliness. God's men have always been lonely men. They have lived alone and liked it. Noah was not invited out to all the social functions of his day. Noah stood alone for God. Abraham may have been the most popular man in Ur of the Chaldees. It was a city with a high civilization. Archaeology tells us that life in Ur of the Chaldees was pleasant in Abraham's day. Undoubtedly he had many friends and was successful in business. One day God called him. And, my friend, it meant loneliness for that man for the rest of his life.

Daniel was in a foreign court, which was bad enough, but this man took a stand for God. Probably no man has ever lived a more lonely life than did Daniel.

Saul of Tarsus may have been the most popular Pharisee in Jerusalem. But Saul of Tarsus one day met Jesus Christ, and that man walked alone during the rest of his life.

Martin Luther had a great many things to take into consideration when the truth of justification by faith broke over his soul. When he looked about him, he saw that all of his friends were on the opposite side. One day that man took a stand for God, and it paid. He made this statement later on, "One with God is a majority."

My friend, to the man or the woman who will take a stand for Jesus Christ and will face the fear of mankind, God says,

**When thou passest through the waters, I will be with thee; and through the rivers, they shall not overflow thee; when thou walkest through the fire, thou shalt not be burned; neither shall the flame kindle upon thee. (Isaiah 43:2)**

**Let your conversation [manner of life] be without**

**covetousness; and be content with such things as ye have; for he hath said, I will never leave thee nor forsake thee.** (Hebrews 13:5)

The Lord Jesus said to His own when He was leaving them and they were to face difficult days,

**I will not leave you comfortless; I will come to you.** (John 14:18)

The word *comfortless* is the Greek word *orphanos*. We get our word *orphans* from that. Jesus said, "I will not leave you orphans—I will come to you." Then He said to them before He left,

**. . . lo, I am with you always, even unto the end of the age. . . .** (Matthew 28:20)

My friend, to be a man-pleaser for fear of loneliness is to deny yourself fellowship with God who will never forsake you and never leave you lonely. Paul, near the end of his life, could write,

**At my first answer no man stood with me, but all men forsook me; I pray God that it may not be laid to their charge. Notwithstanding the Lord stood with me, and strengthened me; that by me the preaching might be fully known, and that all the Gentiles might hear: and I was delivered out of the mouth of the lion.** (2 Timothy 4:16, 17)

Multitudes down through the ages have overcome this awful fear, this fear of loneliness, by
taking a stand for Jesus Christ.

## THE FEAR OF DEATH
## AND JUDGMENT

The fear of death and judgment is the final fear
that I'd like to mention to you. I know that at the
present hour the fact of judgment after death is
called a superstition, that it is considered a hang-
over from the Dark Ages, or that we can dismiss
it as psychological vestigial remains from the Pa-
leozoic period.

My friend, today death and judgment are an
awful reality. You may have your brain washed by
modern thinking, but you never get rid of death
and judgment.

I heard a whimsical story of a man who went
to the psychiatrist. When the psychiatrist asked,
"What's your trouble?" the patient said, "I owe a
man $5,000 and I can't pay it. It has preyed on my
mind so much that I actually think I'm losing my
mind. I can't even sleep at night."

"Have you signed a note?"

"No."

"Was anybody a witness to it?"

"No."

"Well, the thing for you to do is to forget it. Since it has been bothering you, the solution is to get it out of your mind. Now I'm going to rub it out of your mind so you'll actually forget it."

The psychiatrist did such a wonderful job that the fellow got up off the couch and said, "I don't even remember the name of the man that I owe money to." He started to leave.

The psychiatrist said, 'Just a minute. You owe me $50.00 for that treatment."

The man asked, "What treatment?"

My friend, you may not be brainwashed like that, but multitudes of people in this society in which we live *are* brainwashed. And you can't dismiss death and judgment with a wave of the hand. We do well today to fear death and judgment. The Scripture says,

**He, that being often reproved hardeneth his neck, shall suddenly be destroyed, and that without remedy.** (Proverbs 29:1)

Paul went in before Felix, the Roman governor, not to defend himself but to present to him the claims of Christ. The record in Acts 24 says that he reasoned with Felix concerning *righteousness*, the righteousness of Christ; *self-control*, how Christ could control a man; and then the third thing, *judgment to come*. In other words, if Felix turned his back on Jesus Christ, he was going before a holy God, and it would be a frightful eternity ahead of him. Hearing that, Felix trembled with fear and dismissed Paul because he did not want to hear any more about it at all (see Acts 24:25).

The Scripture says, "The fear of the LORD is the beginning of wisdom . . ." (Proverbs 9:10). Fear of the Lord is a reverential fear. It is not a fear which is base or craven. Rather, it is a fear of God that comes through reverence, knowing that our God is a high and holy God and that He must punish sin.

The Scriptures give a beatitude to those who fear the Lord: " . . . Blessed is the man that feareth the LORD . . . (Psalm 112:1). This week I discovered a verse that I don't remember noticing before:

**Happy is the man that feareth alway: but he that hardeneth his heart shall fall into mischief.** (Proverbs 28:14)

It is amazing how up to date that verse is. There's the stimulating stage of fear—"Happy is the man that feareth alway," stimulated by fear and brought to a high and holy God through Christ. "But he that hardeneth his heart shall fall into mischief" is the paralyzing stage, my beloved. One of the things that is said of the apostates in the last days is that they feed themselves without fear:

**These are spots in your feasts of charity, when they feast with you, feeding themselves without fear: clouds they are without water, carried about of winds; trees whose fruit withereth, without fruit, twice dead, plucked up by the roots. (Jude 12)**

Today God has put fear in your heart. That fear, my beloved, can be your salvation, or it can be your undoing. Fear is not something that is always base or craven. If it's a fear of God, it is good. However, if you are fearing men today and living to please them, it is a terrible thing.

I never shall forget the night that word came on the radio that the New London School in East Texas had exploded and that over three hundred boys and girls had been killed. I was speaking the next morning on a radio program in Dallas, Texas, and on that broadcast I directed everything I had to say to the parents and loved ones of those boys and girls. We had cards and letters from New England, from Cuba, from Mexico—from all over the country. A friend of mine, a former schoolmate, was a pastor in the East Texas oil fields at the time of the explosion. He told me this story:

"In the parish in which I was the pastor, there lived a man who had become suddenly rich. He was a Texan who had become oil rich, even had put up a small refinery and had already made several millions of dollars. He had built a lovely home. He had a wife and two fine boys. The wife and two boys were Christians, but the man was the worst blasphemer I have ever met in my life. I've never heard a man talk as that man would talk. He would blaspheme God and curse God. His wife was so concerned about him that she asked me to go see him. I went to see him, and I had never been treated like that in my life—he cursed me from the time I opened my mouth until I got out of earshot. He called me everything that was in the book and some things I didn't know were in the book. He was vile. His wife and one of his little boys took sick during the flu epidemic, and both died at the same time. I went over that night to see him again.

"There sat the father and his one remaining little son. When I went over and sat down beside them and began to talk, he began to abuse me again, and curse—I've never heard anything like it! It was vile beyond description. He repeatedly blasphemed God's name. There was nothing left for me to do but get up and walk out of there, which I did. When I conducted the funeral, the man would not even speak to me. After that experience he became more vile, but all of the love that he had had for his family (and that seemed to be the only thing about the man that was a redeeming feature) was now turned to his little boy who was left.

"Well, that little boy was in the New London School when the explosion occurred. When the man heard of the explosion, he went out to that school and searched through the rubble like a madman until he found the torn and twisted and broken body of his little boy. He took it in his arms and walked up and down that schoolyard like a maniac until someone actually had to take it away from him and take it to the funeral home. You know, I felt it was my duty to go and talk with him, so that night I went over to that big home. I went in, and there was that little white casket, and there he sat in the same place he had sat before. I just steeled myself for the cursing that I was to get. I was afraid to say anything. I just sat down. Then that great big hulk of a fellow looked up—and he hadn't cried before—but now there were tears in his eyes. Instead of cursing me, he said, 'God has been after me all the time. He's tried to speak to me all my life, and I turned my back on Him. He took my wife and my other little boy, and I knew He was talking to me. But I was afraid of what people might say—those I worked with and was associated with. Oh, what a coward I've been! And now God had to take this one. Well, God can have me now.' And that man got down on his knees and took Christ as his Savior."

The last time I saw that pastor friend of mine he told me that the oil man was still serving God.

Friend, today you do well to fear God. But if you trust Him, have committed your life to Him, have taken Him as Savior, then you can say with David,

**The LORD is my shepherd; I shall not want ... Yea, though I walk through the valley of the shadow of death, I will fear no evil: for thou art with me. ...** (Psalm 23:1, 4)

And it's only then that you can experience the truth of the Scripture that says, ". . . Perfect love casteth out fear . . ." (1 John 4:18).

Maybe you have never trusted Christ; or if you have, you have been afraid to take a stand for Him. Has fear filled your heart—fear of men or fear of something else? My friend, bring your fears to God and fear Him. When you fear Him, you will have no one else to fear.

# —7—

# WHAT DO YOU DO WITH YOUR PAST?

Today, as you look back over your shoulder, what do you see? Do you see that which brings joy and satisfaction to your heart? Or do you see that which brings distress, heartbreak, and shame to your life? I'm wondering—are we prepared to make a true assessment, a regular inventory, of this past year, with all of its happenings as far as we are concerned?

Well, there's one axiom that we can lay down for all the years that preceded it: The past is gone, and there is positively nothing that we can do about it.

You and I cannot change one event or one experience.

In a great American drama, one of the first ever written, titled "The Great Divide," one of the leading characters says this, "Wrong is wrong from the moment it happens until the crack of doom, and all the angels in heaven working overtime cannot make it different or less by a half."

May I say to you that this might be true in American drama, but Paul the apostle said that there is something a Christian can do about the past. In fact, Paul made it very personal. Paul said that there was something that *he* did concerning the past. Will you listen to him:

**Brethren, I count not myself to have apprehended: but this one thing I do, forgetting those things which are behind, and reaching forth unto those things which are before, I press toward the mark for the prize of the high calling of God in Christ Jesus. (Philippians 3:13, 14)**

He says, "This *one* thing I do." That is a simple statement of the simple life. In the complex civilization in which we are living, we need to sharpen it down to one point and be able to say, "This *one* thing I do." Most of us today, even in Christian work, are busy with pots and pans as Martha was. We are busy with this and that, and we have quite a few things we are attempting to bring to a boil. But the interesting thing is that we don't seem to be able to watch all of them.

But Paul says, "This *one* thing I do." Call it the power of concentration if you will, or call it the consolidation of purpose, or call it singleness of heart. Call it anything, but it's something that is needed in our Christian lives today. In fact, it is *Bible* all the way through. David said this: "One thing have I desired of the LORD, that will I seek after . . ." (Psalm 27:4). David had reduced his life to the lowest common denominator. In this day of nervous activity, this day of ceaseless motion, this day of building tensions—oh, to reduce our lives down to this one point and be able to say, "This one thing I do."

What is this one thing that Paul did? Well, I lift out only one phrase from Philippians 3:13: "Forgetting those things which are behind." As we look back, there are many things that we are to forget. And this is what Paul did with a great deal of his past.

On the other hand, God gave us memories, and there are certain things we are to remember. As someone has put it, "God gave us memories so that we could have roses in December." The Bible has a great deal to say about remembering. Like a bugle blast, the word *remember* goes all the way through the Word of God. God says to man, "Remember!" He said to the children of Israel, when He brought them out of the land of bondage, "Remember this day, in which ye came out from Egypt, out of the house of bondage . . ." (Exodus 13:3). They were to remember this and never forget it. You find as you go through the Scripture—and it's quite interesting to notice—how the word *remember* is usually associated with God and the word *forget* is associated with man. God is the One who remembers better than we do. You find toward the beginning of Genesis that God remembered Noah. And you find man is constantly forgetting until finally the psalmist sums it all up by saying, "They forgot God their saviour . . ." (Psalm 106:21). And that was tragic. They were not to forget God!

The Scriptures are clear on the fact that to forget certain things is sin. All the way through the

Bible He says to us, "Remember." "Remember now thy Creator in the days of thy youth . . ." (Ecclesiastes 12:1). And even after you leave this life, my beloved, you are still called upon to remember, and you'll remember throughout the endless ages of eternity. It is in Luke 16 that Abraham in sheol said to the rich man yonder in torment, "Remember." And to take a memory like his into eternity, my friend, wouldn't need much fire to make it a hell!

Although there are some things that we are to remember, there are other things that we are to forget. In the biography of Richard III—that villain who wore a crown—the author said of him, "He forgot the things he should have remembered, and he remembered the things he should have forgotten." And how true this is of many of us today. There are certain things we should remember, but there are certain things that we should forget. Many a man goes through life shackled and crippled because he will not forget the things he should forget.

We are not dealing here in generalities. What are some of the things we are to forget? I want to deal with specifics and mention some of them—not all of them, I'm sure—but some of them.

## STUPIDITIES

The first one that I would like to mention is stupidities or blunders. We should forget our blunders. What blunderers we all are, and what blunders we make! Or perhaps I'm wrong in including you. Perhaps you do not commit blunders, but I do. To be frank, we all make blunders, don't we?

Well, let's forget them. In "forgetting the things which are behind," we are to forget our blunders. Sometimes we put our clumsy hands on the heartstrings of a friend and do damage that we did not mean to do. I imagine there are some even today who are saying, "Oh, as I look back over the past year, I said something I wish I had not said. I wish I had bitten off my tongue." Or, "I did something this past year I'm sorry I did. I would not have done it intentionally for anything in the world."

My friend, may I say this to you: Correct what you've done and then forget it! "Forgetting those things which are behind." As you know, Simon Peter was a great blunderer. Matthew 14:28-31 records the incident of Peter walking on water. Peter said to our Lord out yonder on the Sea of Galilee, "Bid me come unto thee on the water." Now don't say that Simon Peter didn't walk on the water because he did. He started out and probably took quite a few steps. But, you see, this fellow was so in the habit of stumbling that he even had to stumble walking on water! He took his eyes off his Lord, saw those boisterous waves and began to sink.

Then you may recall the incident yonder at Caesarea Philippi:

> When Jesus came into the coasts of Caesarea Philippi, he asked his disciples, saying, Whom do men say that I the Son of man am? And they said, Some say that thou art John the Baptist: some, Elias; and others, Jeremias, or one of the prophets. He saith unto them, But whom say ye that I am? And Simon Peter answered and said, Thou art the Christ, the Son of the living God. (Matthew 16:13–16)

Having given that glorious confession of faith, "Thou art the Christ, the Son of the living God," he later opened his mouth and said something he should not have said. In Matthew 16:21–23, when our Lord forewarned the disciples that He was going to Jerusalem to die, Peter took Him aside and rebuked Him. "Be it far from thee, Lord: this shall not be unto thee." What a blunderer!

And then yonder as they left the Upper Room, our Lord said, "This night you will forsake Me. As sheep are scattered, tonight you will be scattered." (See Matthew 26:31–35.) And Simon Peter said, "Though all men shall be offended because of thee, yet will I never be offended." What a blunderer.

But, thank God, this man Peter knew how to get up, dust himself off, forget those things that were behind, and press on to those things which were before him. This man on the day of Pentecost, without mentioning his own base denial, stands up before his countrymen and says,

**Therefore let all the house of Israel know assuredly, that God hath made that same Jesus, whom ye have crucified, both Lord and Christ.** (Acts 2:36)

It brought conviction, and thousands turned to Christ!

May I say to you that Paul also was a blunderer—Peter didn't have a monopoly on it, you know. In Acts 15:36-39 Paul could say in effect, "I don't want John Mark with me. He failed on the first missionary journey, and I will not give him a second chance." It was a mistake not to give John Mark another chance, and there came a day when Paul acknowledged he had been wrong. In his final epistle, his swan song, he wrote: "Take Mark, and bring him with thee, for he is profitable to me for the ministry" (2 Timothy 4:11). Paul blundered, but he corrected it and went on.

## SENSITIVITIES

What is a sensitivity? Well, that's the quality or state of being sensitive. To our stupidities of the past we add our sensitivities.

We are living in an age in which transportation and communication, the increase of population, mass production, and urban life have brought us all together. And we are closer than we have ever been. When you get people close together, they are going to rub against each other. And when you rub any two things together, you get friction. And when you get friction, you get aggravation—and none of the major oil companies have an oil product that will relieve this kind of friction!

Our contemporary society is a hotbed of rivalries and competition and alienations and personality conflicts. In this rough-and-tumble day in which we live, my friend, you are going to get hurt. Somebody is going to offend you. You're bound to be wounded in life's struggle. What are you to do? Oh, how many people up to this present moment are still nursing a grudge and a hurt. Today you may be carrying ill feelings and spreading among God's people disruption and disturbance. What are you to do? Forget them! "Forgetting those things which are behind."

There is a plant that is peculiar to the American continent. It is known as the sensitive plant. Its botanical name is *mimosa pudica*. The characteristic of this little plant is that the minute it is touched by human hand, the stalk withers and the leaves curl up and close tightly.

There are a lot of human beings who are "sensitive plants" in America today. And they come in under the classification of *mimosa pudica*. Oh, my friend, don't let your life be ruined!

In the Bible, the Book of Esther tells about a

man who was like that. His name was Haman. He was a little man, little in mental stature, little in his emotions, little in his character. He was the great anti-Semite, and do you know what teed him off? Well, the king of Persia, Ahasuerus, had elevated Haman to the highest position in the kingdom and had made him prime minister. At the entrance to the city there was a judge, just a petty judge, by the name of Mordecai. Word had been sent around to all the politicians that since Haman had been promoted to such a high office, they were to bow before him. And they all bowed, except that little fellow Mordecai.

Now Mordecai was little physically, but he had great moral courage. He refused to bow. You see, he was a Jew who was true to his God. He had been taught from the Old Testament that he was to worship no one except the Lord his God; so he just would not bow, that was all. You would think that Haman as the prime minister would be big enough to overlook it. But not Haman. Haman went home and complained to his wife—you really find out about a fellow in what he tells his wife! He said to her, "Here the king has lifted me up and made me prime minister, and I am in this exalted position, but I'm not happy because there is a little fellow by the name of Mordecai who won't bow to me!" Because his feelings were hurt, he started a wave of anti-Semitism!

My friend, don't be little. Some people today are bleeders, hemophiliacs, and I am told that the bleeding cannot be stanched. Also some folk are "bleeders" in the social realm. They get pinched or hurt, and they start "bleeding"—and there are not blood transfusions to keep them alive.

Oh, my friend, today as you look back into the past, have you received personal injury? Then forget it. "Forgetting those things which are behind."

## SUCCESSES

There is a third thing that we are to forget: our successes. We are to forget not only our stupidities, not only our sensitivities, but also our successes. Candidly, success is the most difficult of all to forget. Paul could say this: ". . . I have learned, in whatsoever state I am, therewith to be content. I know both how to be abased, and I know how to abound . . ." (Philippians 4:11, 12). To abound, to be successful, is most difficult to forget.

Dr. Harry Ironside used to tell the story of what happened to him in Grand Rapids. He went there every year to speak at Mel Trotter's mission while Mel Trotter was still alive. One year when he went up there, he found that a fine-looking new hotel had been built and that he was booked in this new hotel, up on the top floor in a suite of rooms! He had never had anything like that before. It was luxury personified. He went around just looking at everything in the room, all brand new. He came at last to the door, for they had to publish the price of the room. When Dr. Ironside saw the price, he went immediately to the telephone, called Mel Trotter, and said, "Look, Mel, you don't have to put me in a room like this! If you could just get me a room somewhere with a desk so I can study and a bed for me to sleep in and a washbasin so I can wash my face, that's all I want, and that's all I'm accustomed to." Mel Trotter, in his characteristic manner, said, "Look, Harry, the manager of that hotel was saved several years ago at the mission. He was an alcoholic, a drunk. He's never been able, he says, to repay me. And so when he put up this new hotel, he said, 'I'll reserve the top floor suite for every speaker you have.' Now, Harry, it won't cost me a penny, and it doesn't cost the mission a penny. Learn how to *abound* for the next week."

It is hard to know how to abound, my beloved. Many of us know how to be abased, but very few of us know how to abound. You and I live in a land where success is the watchword. In America we measure a man with the dollar sign. How much money has he made? Has he been a success in business? We measure a man by the schools where he was educated, by his job, and by his influence. My beloved, these values I think are wrong. Many a man is called a success who is a sorry failure at home. Many a person today has a name of fame that makes the headlines but is a rotten failure in marriage.

Do you know that Samuel, one of God's men, was a failure in his home? Oh, I tell you, his life sounds like a success story until you read the following verses that tell of his failure:

**And it came to pass, when Samuel was old, that he made his sons judges over Israel. Now the name of his firstborn was Joel; and the name of his second, Abiah: they were judges in Beer-sheba.**

**And his sons walked not in his ways, but turned aside after lucre, and took bribes, and perverted judgment.** (1 Samuel 8:1–3)

What a failure he was as a father! My brother, if you have made money this past year, if you have attained the position you were after, may I suggest this as a friend: *forget it!* "Forgetting those things which are behind." We do well to forget our successes.

## SORROWS

May I mention the fourth thing briefly. We are not only to forget our stupidities, our sensitivities, and our successes, but we are also to forget our sorrows. Perhaps this past year the death angel knocked at the door of your home—he knocked at many. It may be that tragedy came your way and sorrow fills your heart.

My friend, I do not mean to be pessimistic, but if sorrow did not come, it *will* come. The death angel is no respecter of persons. He knocks at the door of the palace of a pharaoh and the hovel of a peasant. He pays no attention to the status of the individual. He knocks at all doors. He will knock at your door.

If tragedy *did* come your way and sorrow did fill your heart, may I say to you kindly: forget it. "Oh," you say, "you're not asking me to forget my loved one?" No. But forget your sorrow. I receive many letters that ask, "Why did God let this happen to me?" My friend, God let it come to you as a child of God for a definite reason. Will you listen to Him?

**Blessed be God, even the Father of our Lord Jesus Christ, the Father of mercies, and the God of all comfort; who comforteth us in all our tribulation, that we may be able to comfort them which are in any trouble, by the comfort wherewith we ourselves are comforted of God.** (2 Corinthians 1:3, 4)

God has let you, child of God, go down through the valley of the shadow of death in order that He might comfort you. Neither I nor anyone else can comfort you. I disagree with the people who tell me, "You said something that comforted my heart." No, my friend, if your heart was comforted, it was God who did it. He is the God of all comfort.

He alone can comfort you. And He comforts you so that you in turn can go to someone else, and His Word can bring comfort through you.

King David had a little son born to him and, according to the record in 2 Samuel 12, that little one hung in the balance between life and death. David went in before God, fasting. He was down on his face before God, and you could hear him weeping. After a week the little one died, and the servants were afraid to tell David, thinking that he might be so distraught he would do himself bodily harm. David saw that they were whispering and turned and asked, "Is the child dead?" They told him, "Yes." David arose and washed his face, changed his clothes, and went to the house of the Lord and worshiped, then went home and had a good dinner. Even the servants couldn't keep quiet. They came to him and asked, "How is it that when the little one was still alive you fasted and wept, but now that the child is dead you are no longer mourning?" David was God's man, and in concluding his reply he said, "But now he is dead, wherefore should I fast? Can I bring him back again? I shall go to him, but he shall not return to me." In other words, "I'll forget the things that are behind, and I'll move toward the things that are ahead."

Friend, I say it kindly, forget your sorrows.

## SINS

Not only are we to forget our stupidities, our sensitivities, our successes, and our sorrows, but we are to forget our sins, too. What do you do with your sins? The Word of God says to confess them. Confess them promptly to God, and then forget them, my friend, forget them.

I sometimes think that God gets tired of our reminding Him of our past sins. Of course, we are to correct what we have done when we have injured some person. But after we have dealt with the thing and confessed it, He says to forget it— "forgetting those things which are behind." Confession is to be made to God privately—not publicly—and when we have done that, then we are to forget the sin.

Oh, to take the book of the past, tie it with the red ribbon of forgiveness (for that red speaks of the blood of Christ), seal it with love, and then mail it to an address which David gives us: "Shall thy wonders be known in the dark? and thy righteous-ness in the land of forgetfulness?" (Psalm 88:12). I don't know the location of the "land of forgetful-ness." I don't know whether it is north, east, south, or west. Wherever it is, it is the proper place to send the failure of your past—"forgetting those things which are behind."

On the other hand, perhaps your sins are not forgiven, or perhaps you are not *sure* they are for-given. May I ask this personal question? Would you like to wipe out the past, with all of its sins and all of its stains? Would you like to know, as far as your past is concerned, that all is forgiven? Well, God will not only forgive you your sins, friend, He will do something else: He will *forget* them. God says:

> . . . **For I will forgive their iniquity, and I will remember their sin no more.** (Jeremiah 31:34)

> **As far as the east is from the west, so far hath he removed our transgressions from us.** (Psalm 103:12)

God says that He has put our sins behind His back, and He won't turn around. He will forget them.

In closing, let me tell you a story that comes out

of my native state of Texas. Years ago out on the plains of South Texas a ranch house caught on fire one night. Quite suddenly it went up in a blaze. There were a father and mother and several children in that family. All died in the fire with the exception of one little girl about six years old. She came crawling out of that burning inferno, horribly burned on the face. Neighbors took her in. Doctors were called, and they worked with her and nursed her back to health. But the little girl did not have a living relative, so they sent her to Dallas, to the Buckner Orphanage.

Dr. Buckner met her at the train. There she was, a little six-year-old girl all alone, her eyes red with crying and her face horribly scarred. He went up to her and asked, "Are you Mary?"

She said, "Yes. Are you Dr. Buckner? You'll have to be my Daddy and my Mama both. I've lost mine."

He promised he would do his best. He took her out to the home, and she got acquainted with the other children. As you know, sometimes children that age can be rather cruel, even brutal. On one occasion Dr. Buckner had to be out of town, and when he returned all the other children came running, and he put his arms around them and kissed them. Then he saw little Mary standing over to one side. She'd been weeping again, for the children had told her she was ugly. They had told her how horrible she really looked.

So Dr. Buckner went over to little Mary and said to her, "Mary, why didn't you come and kiss Daddy Buckner like the rest?"

"Daddy Buckner, I know I'm ugly. I know I'm awful-looking. You wouldn't possibly want to kiss me. If you'll just say that you love me, that'll be enough."

Do you know what Dr. Buckner with that great heart did? He took her up into his arms, and he kissed those little scarred cheeks. He said to her, "Daddy Buckner loves you just as much as he loves any of these others. You're just as pretty to me as any other."

Oh, my friend, I was that burned child. Sin is what had scarred me. I came to the living God and repented with bitter tears. He forgave me, and through His written Word He said, "I see you in Christ. I accept you in the Beloved. You are lovely to Me. You are My son. You can call Me Father.

And someday you will stand before My throne without spot or blemish."

Friend, we are to forget those things which are behind, and we are to look to Jesus today.

**Looking unto Jesus the author and finisher of our faith; who for the joy that was set before him endured the cross, despising the shame, and is set down at the right hand of the throne of God.** (Hebrews 12:2)

# —8—

# HOW YOU CAN HAVE THE ASSURANCE OF SALVATION

There is a gift which I would like to present to every Christian. It cannot be packed in excelsior, wrapped in bright colored paper, tied with polychrome ribbon, or sealed with good wishes. It cannot be purchased with silver or gold. It is more valuable than all the treasures of this world. All the gold in all the nations of the world could not suffice as a down payment. It is not a material gift of this secular world but a real gift of the spiritual realm. It is intangible, but it is of inestimable and intrinsic value. Many who are rich would pay a handsome sum to possess it. Multitudes strive for it but find it just out of reach. As we face a future filled with fear and foreboding, it might appear as a will-o'-the-wisp. It is desperately and devoutly desired but seldom attained. The world lists this gift as peace of mind and as a feeling of security that all is well for the future. Psychology defines it as a well-integrated personality freed from frustration. Scripture is more specific. The Bible sets forth this gift as a knowledge, a certainty, and an assurance concerning one's personal relationship to God. Simply stated, it is the assurance regarding one's salvation.

Can we know experientially that we are saved and that we are the children of God? For years my soul was tossed on the troubled sea of uncertainty and of insecurity. Finally, there dawned upon my darkened mind the light of Philippians 1:6:

**Being confident of this very thing, that he which hath begun a good work in you will perform it until the day of Jesus Christ.**

It was then that the sun of Scripture rose with many shafts of light and penetrated the dark recesses of my fears and doubts. I pray that I may be given wisdom and power to convey to your fearful heart the assurance of your salvation if it is not already your present possession. For those of you who have experienced the assurance of your salvation, perhaps these few words will stabilize and will strengthen the fabric of your faith. Assurance is your rightful possession, and God wants you to have it as your portion.

First of all, we need to distinguish between a person's eternal security and his assurance of salvation. The line of demarcation must be clearly drawn if we are to enter experientially into the joy of salvation.

Eternal security is an objective fact; assurance of salvation is a subjective experience.

Eternal security is not in the realm of experience; therefore it is totally independent of a person's feelings.

Assurance of salvation is truly an experience. It is an inner consciousness and confidence that a right relationship exists between the soul and God.

Eternal security rests upon certain objective facts which are established and sure; it depends upon God's faithfulness. A simple illustration will clarify this point. The Battle of Bunker Hill is a fact in American history. You and I did not experience the Battle of Bunker Hill, and our feelings are, therefore, no guide to the accuracy of history concerning it.

Eternal security rests upon what God says:

**He that hath the Son hath life; and he that hath not the Son of God hath not life.** (1 John 5:12)

The most wonderful statement in the Bible, or out of the Bible for that matter, is Romans 8:1—

**There is therefore now no condemnation to them which are in Christ Jesus. . . .**

In conjunction with this verse are verses 33 and 34 in the same chapter:

**Who shall lay any thing to the charge of God's elect? It is God that justifieth.**

The throne of God is behind every sinner who has trusted in Jesus.

**Who is he that condemneth? It is Christ that died, yea rather, that is risen again, who is even at the right hand of God, who also maketh intercession for us.**

Christ's work of redemption is adequate enough to secure the perfect salvation for the sinner who trusts Him. If not, then the work of Christ was of no avail, and it was not a *finished* transaction but must be written down as "unfinished business." However in John 19:30 He, as it were, wrote over His cross, "It is finished."

God is offering eternal life—everlasting life—to those who believe in Christ. It is not temporary or uncertain. It is not paid for on the installment plan. It is a gift the moment one believes, but for longer than a moment—for eternity.

You may or you may not have the assurance of this salvation which God offers as everlasting life. There is an anomalous situation which exists to-day. Some Christians believe in the security of the believer but do not themselves have the assurance of their salvation; "Brethren, these things ought not to be," but they do exist.

God wants you to know that you are His child through faith in Jesus Christ:

> **But as many as received him, to them gave he power to become the sons of God, even to them that believe on his name: which were born, not of blood, nor of the will of the flesh, nor of the will of man, but of God.** (John 1:12, 13)

It is not honoring to Him for you to have misgivings, doubts, and a lack of assurance. "Maybe" and "perhaps" should not be in the vocabulary of a born-again Christian when the matter of salvation is the subject. It is not a "hope so" but a "know so" salvation which God offers. It is always described as everlasting or eternal life; it is not temporary or conditional. Listen to God and be assured:

> **He that hath the Son hath life; and he that hath not the Son of God hath not life. These things have I written unto you that believe on the name of the Son of God; that ye may know that ye have eternal life, and that ye may believe on the name of the Son of God.** (1 John 5:12–13)

> **Let us draw near with a true heart in full assurance of faith, having our hearts sprinkled from an evil conscience, and our bodies washed with pure water.** (Hebrews 10:22)

This is not the language of uncertainty. There is a remarkable passage in this connection expressed in Isaiah 32:17:

> **And the work of righteousness shall be peace; and the effect of righteousness quietness and assurance for ever.**

The righteousness which is mentioned here is not man's, but it is the righteousness of God revealed in the gospel. This is the righteousness of Christ which is made over to us and one which gives us a standing before God. It cannot be improved upon because it is perfect, and it cannot be disturbed because it is given to the lost sinner who trusts in Jesus.

God wants all who trust the work of Christ to come to a place in experience where each can say with confidence, boldness, and much assurance, but with true humility:

> . . . **I know whom I have believed, and am persuaded that he is able to keep that which I have committed unto him against that day.** (2 Timothy 1:12)

To fall short of this goal is to miss the best that He has for us. It reveals a defect in our understanding and in our appreciation of His "so great salvation."

A very simple and homely illustration will show that God wants us to enjoy and to be assured of our salvation. Traveling by air is something which I do only in an emergency. Candidly, I have never enjoyed an airplane trip. I lack assurance and confidence in this method of travel. Pictures of train wrecks and statistics of highway fatalities do not increase my relish for air travel. A trip from Los Angeles, California, to Phoenix, Arizona, several years ago to speak at a Youth for Christ meeting and then to hurry back to my Sunday morning service did not increase my love for this mode of travel.

On the way over and on the way back, the trip to me was hazardous. It was a summer Saturday morning on the way over. The intense heat of the desert was threading its way into the cool fog of Southern California between the San Jacinto and San Gorgonio mountains. The plane hit rough air and began to bounce around. Then the pilot found that the higher he went the rougher it got; he leveled off and went through the pass at what looked to be about 10,000 feet. At times the plane would drop, and it seemed to me that it would never stop. I grabbed the seat in front of me and held on for dear life. Of course, the seat in front of me was dropping just as fast as the one in which I was sitting! A fellow traveler aboard, who had been several times around the world by air, stated that this was the roughest trip he had ever experienced. I concurred with him thoroughly, for it surely was my roughest trip—and, as I felt then, my last trip by air. Across the aisle from me sat a young man who was a former pilot. He was asleep by the time the plane took to the air. He was merely annoyed at all the disturbance and turned over and went back to sleep. He had flown many missions over Germany during World War II. When we landed and commented on the rough trip, he simply smiled and confessed that he had enjoyed it all. Frankly, I did not enjoy one minute of it.

Now, I was as safe as this young man. Whatever security the plane offered was mine as well as his. We both had faith enough to enter the plane, but he had the faith, understanding, and experience to enjoy the trip. He had assurance, but I did not. What could have been a pleasant experience for me was a sad ordeal!

My friend, God wants you to enjoy your salvation. His "plane" cannot fall, and you do not have to hold onto the seat in front of you. He holds you!

**My sheep hear my voice, and I know them, and they follow me: and I give unto them eternal life;**

**and they shall never perish, neither shall any man pluck them out of my hand. My Father, which gave them me, is greater than all; and no man is able to pluck them out of my Father's hand.** (John 10:27–29)

He never lets go. Now sit back, relax, and enjoy your salvation. Someone has said, "All the way to heaven is heaven."

## WHY NO ASSURANCE?

There are many reasons why believers do not have the assurance of their salvation. Let us look at some of the principal ones:

*Fear.* Some are frightened souls who received the gospel in trembling and in fear. The gospel was presented partially, and they were not told that they could have any assurance. There is always a serious doubt whether folk like this have ever been saved. The instability and inconsistency of the lives of many who live in the atmosphere of uncertainty do not reveal a thoroughgoing conversion. It is interesting to note what Paul wrote to the

Thessalonians concerning the preaching of the gospel in their city:

**For our gospel came not unto you in word only, but also in power, and in the Holy Ghost, and in much assurance; as ye know what manner of men we were among you for your sake.** (1 Thessalonians 1:5)

The gospel that produces changed lives comes in *much assurance.* Many who lack assurance are sincere, but they have actually never been born again.

While I was pastor in Pasadena, California, an attractive young couple who had come to us out of a liberal church came to me one Wednesday evening after the service and exclaimed with great joy, "We have received the assurance of our salvation tonight!" The next Wednesday evening they came down smiling after the service and said, "Correction, please, we did not get the assurance of our salvation last week; we got saved."

They were thrilled as they related their experience in going home the week before and getting down on their knees and actually receiving Christ as Savior; this experience gave them assurance.

This is the manner in which God intends the gospel to come to men and women—"in much assurance."

*Emotionalism.* Some depend upon an emotional experience, and they do not have the knowledge of their salvation. The gospel has not been given to them accurately, and they merely rest upon an emotional upheaval. If the experience was significant, then they fall back upon it to fortify their faith. When the emotional experience wears thin and there is not much to rest upon, then doubts and uncertainty creep in to make the heart disturbed. Many of these do not know the assurance that there is in the gospel:

> **That their hearts might be comforted, being knit together in love, and unto all riches of the full assurance of understanding, to the acknowledgement of the mystery of God, and of the Father, and of Christ.** (Colossians 2:2)

Again, permit me to resort to a personal experience to clarify this point. One Easter Sunday several years ago, two couples came forward at the invitation. One couple was overcome with emotion; the other couple was stoical. The elders who dealt with them could not get a clear statement from the emotional couple because they were weeping so. The contrast was so great that some even doubted the genuineness of the couple who shed no tears. However, time proved that emotion was no indication of a real experience of conversion, for the emotional couple were pulled out of one "ism" shortly after this incident and are at present in a second "ism." Their instability indicates that they will bounce out of this second "ism," but the chances are they will soon bounce into a third one. The couple who seemed to have had no experience at all have grown in grace and in the knowledge of Christ. It is a joy to see them take their regular places in the services of the church. This couple had the "full assurance of understanding" from the very beginning.

**Sin.** Sin which is not confessed in the life of a believer is the greatest single factor in robbing him of the assurance of salvation. God wants us to have the full assurance of salvation. God wants us to have the full assurance of faith, and this comes experientially through fellowship with God. Sin breaks our fellowship, and this in time sets up a chain reaction that breaks our assurance.

**If we say that we have fellowship with him, and walk in darkness, we lie, and do not the truth.** (1 John 1:6)

We can bluff our way through before others by putting up a front that all is well. But underneath doubts begin to gnaw like little foxes at the fringe of our faith, and we actually feel that we are not really God's children. We dread the light because it makes us more conscious of our doubts. God is still our Father nonetheless, and a conviction of sin is pretty good evidence. We have lost our fellowship—not our salvation.

The Christian should come to the light which is the Word of God. It reveals our sin but it likewise shows us the remedy. The blood of Christ is still potent, and it is the basis of forgiveness for the sins of a child of God.

**But if we walk in the light, as he is in the light, we have fellowship one with another, and the blood of Jesus Christ his Son cleanseth us from all sin.** (1 John 1:7)

The believer who walks in the light and who discovers sin in his life knows that the blood of Christ keeps on cleansing him from sin; consequently, he goes in confession to Him:

**If we confess our sins, he is faithful and just to forgive us our sins, and to cleanse us from all unrighteousness.** (1 John 1:9)

Immediately fellowship is restored for the sinning saint. The family fellowship is resumed and confidence and assurance are restored. You see, the child of God is always disturbed by sin in his life as he knows it breaks fellowship with God. In fact, the line of demarcation is drawn at this point between God's children and the devil's offspring:

**In this the children of God are manifest, and the children of the devil: whosoever doeth** [practices] **not righteousness is not of God, neither he that loveth not his brother.** (1 John 3:10)

Deliberate and continual sinning without remorse or without repentance is a clear indication that one has not come into the place of sonship. The child of God is distressed, disturbed, and distraught by the presence of sin in his life. He hates the sin in his life and longs to be delivered from it. The presence of sin robs him of his assurance. The legitimate child of God can never compromise with the sin in his life. The child of God longs to obey God and to please Him:

**And hereby we do know that we know him, if we keep his commandments.** (1 John 2:3)

This desire to obey God gives him an assurance that he is a son of God. He wants to know the will of God, and therefore he wants to know the Word of God. He goes then where he can hear the Word of God:

**I rejoice at thy word, as one that findeth great spoil.** (Psalm 119:162)

**I hate vain thoughts: but thy law do I love.** (Psalm 119:113)

**O how love I thy law! it is my meditation all the day.** (Psalm 119:97)

He finds that he not only has an appetite for the Word of God, but he also begins to understand it and thereby growth takes place:

**But he that is spiritual judgeth** [understands] **all things, yet he himself is judged** [understood] **of no man.** (1 Corinthians 2:15)

## HOW CAN I KNOW?

There are other tests which indicate to a trembling but trusting heart that he or she is a child of God. God urges us to make the tests so that we may have assurance:

**Examine yourselves, whether ye be in the faith; prove your own selves. Know ye not your own selves, how that Jesus Christ is in you, except ye be reprobates?** (2 Corinthians 13:5)

Here are some of the tests:

*A reality in prayer* is an evidence that we are children of God. There is a very remarkable statement in this connection made in 1 John 3:19–22:

**And hereby we know that we are of the truth, and shall assure our hearts before him.**

As the child of God approaches the Father, a holy boldness confirms the heart. This is not presumption on the part of the child—it is the assurance that a child has in approaching a father. However, sin or some other impediment may make us hesitant and reluctant to approach the Father. God does not hear us because of our reluctance but because of Christ, and He hears us regardless of our condition:

> **For if our heart condemn us, God is greater than our heart, and knoweth all things.**

Nevertheless, when our hearts are rightly related to Him, then there is a confidence given to us:

> **Beloved, if our heart condemn us not, then have we confidence toward God.**

Furthermore, when we are in His will, there are added tokens that we are His children:

> **And whatsoever we ask, we receive of him, because we keep his commandments, and do those things that are pleasing in his sight.**

Answered prayer is an argument that we are legitimate children of God. The prayer-life of the believer is vital in assuring the soul of salvation.

*A love for the brethren* gives evidence that we are children of God. One of the most convicting and confirming facts which seals assurance to the heart is love of the brethren. Scripture is positive at this point:

**We know that we have passed from death unto life, because we love the brethren. He that loveth not his brother abideth in death.** (1 John 3:14)

Animosity and hatred in the heart will rob the child of God of assurance. Malice toward another Christian produces bitterness of soul and is therefore not a fertile soil to cultivate assurance. Malice is condensed anger. Lack of love for another believer probably robs more Christians of real enjoyment and satisfaction in the Christian life than does any other single factor. It not only blights the soul of the Christian, but it also destroys any public testimony:

**By this shall all men know that ye are my disciples, if ye have love one to another.** (John 13:35)

To love other believers is not elective:

**These things I command you, that ye love one another.** (John 15:17)

Do not let a little root of bitterness rob you of assurance. Make things right with other believers.

Not only will we who are believers love those within the Christian fellowship, but we will also have a desire for those outside the fold to come to a saving knowledge of Christ. A sterile and frigid Christian is not likely to experience the sweetness and joy of full assurance, but a vital Christian, who knows something of the Savior's compassion, will find the joy of belonging and an abiding experience.

*A consciousness that we are children of God* comes to the soul, and it is another evidence that we are the sons of God. This is the gracious work of the Spirit of God and not the product of psychological presumption.

> **Hereby know we that we dwell in him, and he in us, because he hath given us of his Spirit.** (1 John 4:13)

This does not mean that we are conscious of the presence of the Holy Spirit, but it does mean that we are conscious of the work of the Holy Spirit. The Holy Spirit does not speak of Himself, but He speaks of Christ:

> **Howbeit when he, the Spirit of truth, is come, he will guide you into all truth: for he shall not speak of himself; but whatsoever he shall hear, that shall he speak: and he will show you things to come.** (John 16:13)

Part of the work of the Holy Spirit is to make us conscious that we are the children of God.

**The Spirit itself** (Himself) **beareth witness with our spirit, that we are the children of God.** (Romans 8:16)

There is a counterfeit humility which is going the rounds today and it sounds very pious, but it does not have the ring of the genuine. Some say that we are to grovel in the dust and that we are to act like worms—this is the modern way of putting on sackcloth and ashes. It is true that we *are* sinners; there is no good within us, no good comes out of us, and we have nothing in which to glory save the cross of Christ. Nevertheless, the Holy Spirit does not bear witness with our spirit that we are the "worms" of God. No, He encourages us when we are in times of weakness and trembling, and in spite of all our failure He assures us that we are children of God.

And a remarkable thing is stated in the preceding verse:

**For ye have not received the spirit of bondage again to fear; but ye have received the Spirit of adoption, whereby we cry, Abba, Father.** (Romans 8:15)

The word *Abba* is an untranslated Aramaic word. The translators of the first English Bibles, who had great reverence for the Word of God, who believed it was indeed the Word of God, would not translate it. *Abba* is a very personal word that could be translated "My Daddy." We don't use this word in reference to God because of the danger of becoming overly familiar with Him. But the Spirit affirms it and causes us to realize that God is our very own Father through regeneration and by adoption.

While I was praying one morning shortly before Christmas, my little seven-year-old daughter tiptoed into the room and placed a letter before me. Since I was getting nowhere in my prayer, I paused to read the contents of the letter which she had scribbled in her childish hand. (See page 183.)

Before Christmas, a father always comes into his proper position in the home and is treated with due respect. Nevertheless, the letter caused me to drop to my knees and to be conscious anew and afresh that God was my Father. I cried out in joy, "You are my Father, and I love You. You have been gracious to me, and I know You always will." The veil was removed from my eyes, and my soul was

DeaR DADDY
I LoVe you
you HAVe
Bin KinDto
me AnDI
hoPE you WiLL
KeeP on
Being KinD
to me
Love
LynDA

flooded with a fresh consciousness that I was a son of God. This was the gracious work of the Spirit of God.

There is an experience of salvation for the child of God that he does not have to seek. It will come, for it is impossible for the Holy Spirit to regenerate a sinner and for Christ to dwell in the heart and there not be a corresponding experience.

Dr. George Truett told a story out of his long and fruitful ministry at the First Baptist Church in Dallas, Texas. One day he had the sad office of conducting the funeral of a young wife and mother from his congregation. After the service, friends gathered around the young husband and the little girl who were left. The friends urged the father to go with them to their homes for a few days. He refused with the statement that he would have to face the reality of life without his wife, and he would begin at once. He took the little girl back to the lonely house where everything in it reminded him of his wife. The little girl, sensing that something was wrong but not old enough to appreciate the situation, kept calling for her mother. The child did not make it any easier by constantly reminding the father that he was not feeding her or putting her to bed as her mother was accustomed to do. When the father had finally tucked the little one in bed and he was in bed thinking the little girl was asleep, he cried aloud in his anguish of soul, "O God, it is dark down here."

The child was not asleep and began to cry and to say, "Daddy, it is dark over here, too. Take me in bed with you." The father took the little one in bed with him and attempted to soothe her sobbing. Then she reached over in the darkness and felt the face of her father. "Daddy," she said, "I can go to sleep if your face is toward me." Being assured that his face was toward her, she soon dropped off into peaceful slumber.

The anxious father thought over this incident and the simple faith of the child in him as a father. Then he cried out again, "O God, it is dark down here, but I can bear it if I know Your face is toward me." Soon he too was sound asleep. The Holy Spirit in a time of darkness and emergency confirms to the sad spirit of the child of God that he is a son of God and that the Heavenly Father does not have His face averted from His own.

Perhaps these words have not been convincing to many anxious souls because they cannot establish with any degree of certainty a moment in time when they had a transforming experience with God. But there does not have to be a date for a "second birthday." Multitudes are kept in uncertainty because they hear others testify to a day, a moment, and a place when they passed from death to life. If you have had such an experience, it certainly must be gratifying. But many others have not, yet they also are born-again believers.

If I may be permitted a final personal reference,

this is my experience. I have never been able to put my finger on the moment that I was converted. As a boy, I went to an altar under a brush arbor, but no one thought to speak to me about my soul or to explain the way of salvation. The devil formerly used this to disturb my mind when I heard someone testify to a transforming experience. It seemed that he would lean over my shoulder and whisper, "How do you know that you have accepted Christ?"

Dr. Lewis Sperry Chafer gave me the solution to this problem in a class lecture when I was in seminary, and the devil does not disturb me on this anymore. Now I say to him, "Perhaps, you are right. I may never have accepted Christ in the past. But you are witness that here and now I accept Him with all my heart. Now I am a child of God." If this has been your difficulty, then I beseech you to accept Christ this very moment—assure your heart and have the peace of God.

Do not look for an experience! Do not probe your feelings! Do not use psychoanalysis! Believe God! Take Him at His Word! Trust His faithfulness! "Let God be true and every man a liar."

Christ says in John 6:37, " . . . Him that cometh to me, I will in no wise cast out." Will you come?

**He that hath the Son hath life; and he that hath not the Son of God hath not life.** (1 John 5:12)

# — 9 —

# HOMESICK FOR HEAVEN

**Being therefore always of good courage, and knowing that, whilst we are at home in the body, we are absent from the Lord (for we walk by faith, not by sight); we are of good courage, I say, and are willing rather to be absent from the body, and to be at home with the Lord.** (2 Corinthians 5:6–8, ASV)

Well, where is this home, and what is this home like? We are going to stand on the fringe and peer over the wall into a vast domain. We are going to look out upon the seemingly rolling waves of an endless sea that is this subject of heaven. We're told here that we are to be "at home with the Lord." This is one of the lovely expressions—and Scripture is filled with these lovely expressions—that speak of the eternal state of the believer, "at home with the Lord."

Now this fifth chapter of 2 Corinthians is one of the highlights of the Word of God. It is of paramount importance to the careful student of the Bible. There is here a presentation of many different subjects which are arresting, intriguing, and impressive.

The interesting thing is that for some of them no conclusion is reached. A problem is stated but not adequately answered—or perhaps not answered to our satisfaction. For instance, the apostle Paul writes, "For we know that if our earthly house of this tabernacle were dissolved, we have a building of God, an house not made with hands, eternal in the heavens" (2 Corinthians 5:1). Does he mean there is a temporary body given to us when we leave this earth, before we receive our new body? There are many expositors who take that position.

Then we are told here about the judgment seat

of Christ. "For we must all appear before the judgment seat of Christ; that every one may receive the things done in his body, according to that he hath done, whether it be good or bad" (2 Corinthians 5:10). There has always been a question about how much of our Christian life is going to be exposed at this judgment. I have always felt that it will be put on the screen like a motion picture and that no detail will be left out. But this concept could be entirely wrong.

Then in 2 Corinthians 5:17 we learn that if we are in Christ, we are a new creation: "Therefore if any man be in Christ, he is a new creature: old things are passed away; behold, all things are become new." How much is involved in that?

Then God opens up the great subject of reconciliation.

**And all things are of God, who hath reconciled us to himself by Jesus Christ, and hath given to us the ministry of reconciliation; to wit, that God was in Christ, reconciling the world unto himself, not imputing their trespasses unto them; and hath committed unto us the word of reconciliation.** (2 Corinthians 5:18, 19)

I do not think anyone has been able to probe the depths of that great theme.

Finally, we are told that we are ambassadors:

**Now then we are ambassadors for Christ, as though God did beseech you by us: we pray you in Christ's stead, be ye reconciled to God.** (2 Corinthians 5:20)

What is involved in being an ambassador for Christ? We know some things, but there are other things apparently we do not know.

## HEAVEN—WHERE IS IT?

Now for this message we are going to restrict ourselves to one of these suggestive subjects—that is, it will not be adequate nor will it be all-comprehensive, only suggestive.

We are told here, as we are told elsewhere in the Word of God, that there is a heaven out in space. This is a revelation found in the New Testament.

It's not the hope of the Old Testament. As far as I can tell from the Old Testament, God never told anyone that He was going to remove them from this earth to a place out yonder that we call heaven. He did say that our earth would become the Kingdom of Heaven, and I understand this to be the full and adequate meaning of that expression.

"The Kingdom of Heaven" is a progressive term, I grant that, but its final fruition will be the establishment of God's kingdom on this earth, and that means this earth will become heaven or a portion of God's heaven. Now that was the hope of the Old Testament, but it's not the hope of the New Testament.

The first mention of God taking a group of people from this earth out into space is mentioned by our Lord in the Upper Room. This One who had been the carpenter of Nazareth down here, said to His own,

> . . . I go to prepare a place for you. And if I go and prepare a place for you, I will come again, and receive you unto myself; that where I am, there ye may be also. (John 14:2, 3)

And Paul, banking on that statement, wrote that to be absent from the body is to be at home with the Lord.

Now what about this place? Paul confirmed its

existence, but the only description I can find of it is in the twenty-first chapter of the Book of Revelation. Therefore, we will have to go there to get the description of this wonderful place where we are to be at home.

We should note that our knowledge of it brings courage and comfort to the heart, and I am sure that one of the reasons so many of God's people have become discouraged along life's pathway is because they've lost sight of the place where they are going. If you've read John Bunyan's *Pilgrim's Progress* which, by the way, was his own experience, you will find that this man Christian, though he went down into the Slough of Despond or went down into Doubting Prison, always could come out and face the future and move upward on the pilgrim pathway because, as he says, "I am on the way to the Celestial City."

Many of God's children are so wrapped up in this world today, like a kitty in a ball of yarn, that they have lost sight of the fact that we are pilgrims and strangers down here and that to look forward to the Celestial City also brings courage and comfort to the heart in our day.

Now we want to turn to chapter 21 of the Book

of Revelation. And as we do, we want to see the description that is given here. We find that there are two features we want to develop at this time:

First is the *top*ography of heaven. And second is the *typ*ography of heaven. These are the two themes, the topography of heaven and the typography of heaven.

Now first of all, when we speak of the topography of heaven, we mean that it is a place, a material place, if you please. I do not know why there has come in a notion today that the difference between that which is spiritual and that which is carnal means the difference between the material, which you can see, and that which you can't see, which has no physical qualities whatsoever. That is not true. Actually, some of the most carnal things in this world are things you can't see. Hate and covetousness are works of the flesh, but they are just as much in the spiritual realm as love and unselfishness, which are the fruit of the Spirit.

On the other hand, a thing does not have to be out yonder in space with no existence to be spiritual, my beloved. Heaven is a good example of this because it is a place with three dimensions: it has height, it has width, it has depth—all of these things. Yet it is in the realm of the spirit.

Notice the description of heaven that is given. And may I say again—I continually repeat it—that the interpretations I am giving you are only suggestions. Yet I trust if you have become discouraged or perhaps you have not yet begun the pilgrim pathway to this city, that you will be encouraged by what is given here.

**And I saw a new heaven and a new earth: for the first heaven and the first earth were passed away; and there was no more sea.** (Revelation 21:1)

This tells us that there will come into existence a new heaven and a new earth. God is trading in this model on a new one, one that will be absolutely, of course, free of sin. And the only change that is called to our attention is the fact that there will be no sea. What a great change that will be!

Now we in Los Angeles are thankful for the ocean. If you do not see why, then take a trip 200 miles to the east or go to Chicago, and you'll see why the ocean is such a valuable asset here on the West Coast.

But can you conceive of this earth without any

ocean, that which occupies three-fourths of the globe's surface? If now we had all that space, what a tremendous population could be put here—and will be put here in the eternal ages. Not only that, just think of the parking space we're going to have when we get rid of the ocean! "No more sea" is the one radical change we are told about. Then God moves on and tells about something else that will be new.

Up to this point heaven has been mentioned many times in Scripture, but never described. Our Lord said He was going to prepare a place for us in it; Paul wrote about being homesick for it and wanting to go there; and now it comes into view for the first time. I think it's already in existence, but I don't think we're going to see it until eternity begins; that is, until we have the new heaven and a new earth.

Now will you notice what he says,

**And I John saw the holy city, new Jerusalem, coming down from God out of heaven, prepared as a bride adorned for her husband.** (Revelation 21:2)

It is a holy city and it's holy because there is no sin there at all. Those who are there are clothed in the righteousness of Christ, and they are in Him, they're His bride, and that's the reason it's a holy city. It is the new Jerusalem, because it's in contrast to an earthly Jerusalem.

And then the loveliest thing of all is said concerning it here, that this city is as a bride adorned for her husband. Now I can't think of any figure of speech that's more adequate than that, "as a bride adorned for her husband."

It has been my privilege in my ministry to have about 200 couples stand before me to be married. And I must confess that I still enjoy standing down in front with the bridegroom. I want to say he is generally not much to look at, but I stand with him, and both of us together are probably not much to look at.

But as we stand there, I always look in anticipation—not as he does of course—but I look in anticipation to see the bride. And I want to say as I've seen them come down the aisle, and I'm prepared to make this statement and stand by it, I have never yet seen an ugly bride. Every one that I have seen has been beautiful and some of them absolutely ravishing, but they are all beautiful.

Now you say, "The trouble with you, Preacher,

is that you're getting in your dotage and you're becoming just a little sentimental." And in case you think I'm becoming sentimental, I want to say that I have seen these girls, many of them, before they got married. In fact, I've been at the rehearsal when they had these curlers on. And I want to tell you that beauty was not the way to speak of them. And then I want to say I've seen them after they've been married. And you can't always say they're beautiful. But for some reason, God permits every girl to be beautiful on her wedding day. Yes, He does. I've never seen it fail.

Now, my beloved, I think this is the loveliest thing that can be said about the city. This city is a thing of beauty; it is as a bride adorned for her husband. After all, the church is the bride of Christ and coming with the Bridegroom. And this is certainly an adequate picture of it.

## TOPOGRAPHY

Now I want you to look at the topography of this city, and it's given to us here. It comes down, we're told, from God out of heaven. It comes down into space, but we are not told it comes to the earth.

There are some very fine expositors today who take the position that it comes to this earth. I personally believe that it stays in space. And we're told,

**And the city lieth foursquare, and the length is as large as the breadth: and he measured the city with the reed, twelve thousand furlongs. The length and the breadth and the height of it are equal.** (Revelation 21:16)

Two facts are evident from this passage: it comes down out of heaven, and it is not stated that it comes to the earth. The passage of Scripture leaves the city hanging in mid air. That is the dilemma many expositors seek to avoid, but why not leave the city in mid air? Is there anything incongruous about a civilization in space?

When I first wrote this theory and it appeared in print, it was really out of keeping with our limited knowledge of space during those years. However today a rendezvous in space is not something that is strange at all.

We are told that this city lieth foursquare, that it is approximately 1500 miles on each side. There are expositors today who think the city is shaped as a cube. There are others who think of it shaped as a pyramid. Candidly, I would say that either one of these would be rather awkward out in space. I don't mean to say it would be impossible, but I've always felt that there might be some other explanation.

Now what I am going to say is only a theory—please keep that in mind.

The measurements of the city have given rise to all sorts of conceptions as to the size and shape of the city. First of all, notice the size of the city: twelve thousand furlongs are given as the measurement of each side and of the height. It is 12,000 stadia in the text, which means about 1500 miles.

Now consider with me the shape of the city. "The city lieth foursquare" is the simple declaration of Scripture. That would seem to indicate that the city is a cube with 1500 miles on a side—that is, 1500 miles long, 1500 miles wide, and 1500 miles high. Students of Scripture interpret these measurements in many geometric figures, a cube or pyramid, etc. However it is difficult to conceive of either a cube or a pyramid projected out in space. We are accustomed to think of a sphere hanging in space because that is the general shape

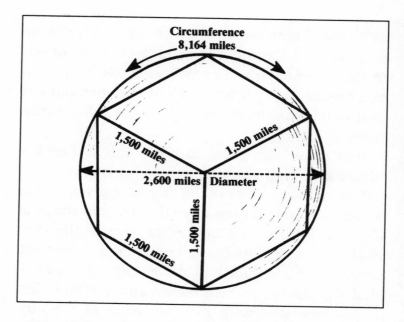

of heavenly bodies. Yet it is definitely stated that the city is foursquare.

The difficulty resolves when we think of the city as a cube within a crystal-clear sphere. Several times attention is called to the fact that the city is like a crystal-clear stone or crystal-clear gold. This emphasis leads us to believe that the city is seen through the crystal. We live on the outside of the planet called earth, but the bride will dwell within the planet called the New Jerusalem. The glory of light streaming through this crystal-clear prism will break up into a polychromed rainbow of breathtaking beauty. The sphere will have the circumference of 8164 miles. The diameter of the moon is about 2160 miles, and that of the New Jerusalem sphere is about 2600 miles; thus the New Jerusalem will be about the size of the moon. And it will be a sphere, as are the other heavenly bodies.

Some folk are interested in going to the moon. Well, I'm going to wait until this one appears in space because this will be my home someday. And I'm very much interested in it since I intend to spend eternity there.

Now I believe this is the reason you have description given of the street of gold, and it says it's clear gold. Man has perfected through processes of metallurgy different colors of gold—yellow, green, white gold; but we are not yet seeing transparent gold. However the gold of the New Jerusalem is like clear glass. The city is translucent, but the material is gold in contrast to the crystal-clear stone that surrounds the city. Why should it be clear and what difference does it make about the asphalt we walk on? It's clear because light is coming from the inside out.

I believe that you and I live in a universe that is actually dark. It has "light holders" in it, but space out there is dark and cold. And one day God will push a button, as it were, and just like you turn off the lights in your home, God will push a button and every sun will go out of existence. He says here,

> **And the city had no need of the sun, neither of the moon, to shine in it: for the glory of God did lighten it, and the Lamb is the light thereof.** (Revelation 21:23)

Our Lord will be in this city, and His light will go out through that twelve-stone foundation. What a thing of beauty! Look at those twelve stones, each one a different color. Varied hues and tints form a galaxy of rainbow colors:

1. Jasper (*iaspis*), the diamond, crystal-clear, a reflector of light and color.
2. Sapphire (*sappheiros*), blue, "as the body of heaven in its clearness."
3. Chalcedony (*chalkedon*), greenish agate stone (we don't know the exact color of all of these precious stones).

4. Emerald (*smaragdos*), green.
5. Sardonyx (*sardonux*), red and white stone.
6. Sardius (*sardios*), fiery red.
7. Chrysolite (*chrusolithos*), golden yellow.
8. Beryl (*berullos*), sea green.
9. Topaz (*topazion*), greenish-yellow.
10. Chrysoprasus (*chrusoprasos*), gold-green.
11. Jacinth (*huakinthi*), color of a hyacinth.
12. Amethyst (*amethustos*), purple.

The New Jerusalem is a city of light and a city of color. "God is light" and He is there. The city is described as a jasper stone and clear as crystal. The jasper stone is a sphere and the city, New Jerusalem, is within. The light shining from within through the jasper stone, acting as a prism, would give every color and shade of color in the rainbow city of Jerusalem. The New Jerusalem is a new planet, and the city is inside a crystal ball. The presence of the primary colors suggests that every shade and tint is reflected from that city. A rainbow that appears after a summer shower gives only a faint impression of the beauty in coloring of the city of light. Our universe that's rather drab and cold and dark today will really be flooded with light. It will be the most thrilling sight in the world to see Him turn out all the lights and then this one will go on in the new heaven and the new earth!

The New Jerusalem will be a holy place:

**And the nations of them which are saved shall walk in the light of it: and the kings of the earth do bring their glory and honour into it. And the gates of it shall not be shut at all by day: for there shall be no night there. And they shall bring the glory and honour of the nations into it. And there shall in no wise enter into it any thing that defileth, neither whatsoever worketh abomination, or maketh a lie: but they which are written in the Lamb's book of life.** (Revelation 21:24–27)

The nations of the earth will make a trip up here—they'll make a trip in space. The New Jerusalem is the holy of holies of the universe just as there was a holy of holies in the temple. The high priest didn't stay there—he performed his service then he left.

And the people of the earth will come up here to worship, bringing their glory and honor. They're not going to stay because it is not their home. This is the home of the church, and this is where all those who are in Christ will be at home with the Lord.

A place like this, may I say, is one of the most thrilling places to look at, but actually, that is not the chief function of the city.

## TYPOGRAPHY

There is something else. Not only do we try to apprehend the topography of heaven, but notice the typography of heaven. And here our Lord uses terms of accommodation. In other words, it's difficult for you and me to get our thinking adjusted to the way heaven really will be. Therefore, He uses terminology that is typical, and here are examples of it. These are things beyond our experience that He mentions. You will notice several of them, and we will not attempt to be exhaustive but simply, again, make some suggestions to stimulate your thinking.

## NO TEARS

**And God shall wipe away all tears from their eyes; and there shall be no more death, neither sorrow,**

**nor crying, neither shall there be any more pain: for the former things are passed away.** (Revelation 21:4)

Now that is something that you and I have never seen—a world or a city or a community or a home or a person who has never shed a tear.

Ours is a world that's filled with tears. A book on anthropology that was quoted recently in the newspaper has this statement which interests me a great deal. Of course, the author uses the terminology of the anthropologist:

Man is the only animal born into this world that cannot take care of himself. He cannot protect himself, he cannot sustain himself. The only thing he can do when he comes into this world is cry.

That's all he does on his own, and that's the first thing he does. He makes his entrance into this world crying, and he makes it loud and long, for you and I are in a world filled with tears.

Now tears are the badge of heartbreak, homebreak, and disappointment. We are in that kind of world today. Won't it be wonderful to be in a city—regardless of its shape—where there will be no more tears? The apostle Paul wrote,

**Paul and Timotheus, the servants of Jesus Christ, to all the saints in Christ Jesus which are at Philippi, with the bishops and deacons:... For I am in a strait betwixt two, having a desire to depart, and to be with Christ; which is far better.** (Philippians 1:1, 23)

To be at home with the Lord means no more tears, never again a tear. As a pastor, I've seen too many of them. We never miss a week without seeing tears. I saw them this week again—heartbreak! Oh, my beloved, this world, as an agnostic said, is a veil of tears. From his viewpoint, that's exactly what it is, a veil of tears. And I tell you, unless you are a pilgrim and stranger down here and headed for the celestial city where our Lord is going to wipe away all tears, you are apt to become very discouraged.

## NO DEATH

Now will you notice a second thing which is beyond our experience: "And there shall be no more death." Death is something that is prevalent in this world today—"in Adam all die." There's not a city today or any community that does not have a cemetery. One of the many, multitudinous problems of Southern California is to get a place to bury people. That's a real problem today. It will be wonderful to be in a city in which that's no problem at all because there will be no one dying. There will be no more death. Aren't you tired of going to the cemetery? I think every pastor will be glad not to have to make another trip out there. That would be wonderful. The undertaker is going to be out of business, the cemetery will be out of business. And when I mentioned this some time ago, a little boy sitting next to his father in the congregation said, "Dad, not only the undertaker will be out of business, not only will the cemetery be out of business, but you're going to be out of business." His father is an insurance man. He will be out of business also. My beloved, may I say to you, it will be wonderful to be in a place where there is "no more death, neither sorrow, nor crying, neither shall there be any more pain: for the former things are passed away" (Revelation 21:4).

## ALL THINGS NEW

Now we come to that which to me is the high point of the New Jerusalem where we'll be at home with the Lord.

**And he that sat upon the throne said, Behold, I make all things new. And he said unto me, Write: for these words are true and faithful.** (Revelation 21:5)

And the Lord Jesus said in effect, "Let Me sign My Name to this because this is so important: Behold I make all things *new.*"

Does that mean anything to you today? Well, it is a great encouragement to me. I'd like to make a confession to you—I make it readily and gladly—I have never attained my goal in life. I have never been the man that I have wanted to be. I have never been the husband I've wanted to be, nor have I been the father I've wanted to be. And may I say that I have never been the preacher I've wanted to be. I have never yet preached the sermon that I'd like to preach. I have found in my life that there have been hindrances, there have been frustrations, there have been disappointments. I've felt many times that things have been unfair and unjust. Have you felt that way? My Lord says, "Behold, I make all things new."

May I be personal? The Lord Jesus said in effect, "Vernon McGee, you didn't run the race like you wanted to run it. You didn't cross the tapeline as you wanted to cross it. You didn't live as you wanted to live. But we are going to start all over again—behold, I make all things new."

I don't know about you, but I want to do it all over again. Not down here, oh my, no—I don't want to go back over my life. I would never want to do that. But what a glorious prospect to start over again! The apostle Paul wrote, "To be absent from the body is to be at home with the Lord." This is the place our Lord Jesus had reference to when He said,

> ... I go to prepare a place for you. And if I go and prepare a place for you, I will come again, and receive you unto myself. ... (John 14:2,3)

## AT HOME WITH THE LORD—HOW?

Let's come back where we began this message, "At home with the Lord." How are we going to get there? If anyone is in Christ, he is a new creation. Old things are passed away, and all things have become new.

I'm very frank to tell you that I'm not fit for

heaven in this old nature. I don't know why so many of the saints today feel that they're going to adorn heaven when they get there and that they're going to make a tremendous contribution to it. My friend, you and I have no contribution to make to heaven. We have an old nature that is in rebellion against God. We'd like to set up a little kingdom apart from God. We have to be made fit for heaven. And how can we be made fit for heaven?

"If any man be in Christ, he is a new creation: old things. . . ." What does He mean by old things? A few little habits? No, a new relationship. When we are in Christ, we are no longer joined to the old Adam, but now through faith in Christ we are joined to the resurrected, glorified Savior, clothed in His righteousness and made accepted in the Beloved. All of this because of one thing—our faith in Jesus Christ! We walk by faith and not by sight.

**Now then we are ambassadors for Christ, as though God did beseech you by us: we pray you in Christ's stead, be ye reconciled to God.** (2 Corinthians 5:20)

And as long as I'm down here, He is saying to me, "McGee, you're an ambassador for Christ." And as long as there are ambassadors in this world, it means that the government they represent and the ruler is still at peace with the world. One of these days He's calling His ambassadors home and when He does, the door will be shut and the entrance blocked to this city. But until then we are ambassadors for Christ: " . . . as though God did beseech you by us, we pray you in Christ's stead [that is, when the Lord Jesus left, He asked us to implore you] be ye reconciled to God."

The Lord Jesus said,

**I am the way, the truth, and the life; no man cometh unto the Father, but by me.** (John 14:6)

He is the way to that city, "I am the way, the truth and the life, no man cometh unto the Father, but by me." And He made a dead-end street out of all of the other so-called ways to God, and He says, "You can be reconciled because I am reconciled to you." When Christ died on the cross, He did all that was necessary to save you. He said, "It is finished." He turned in His report to the Father and said, "I have finished the work which You have given Me to do" (John 17:4). My friend, you don't have to do anything to add to your salvation. He asks you only to be reconciled to God.

Will you accept it? Will you agree with God that this is the way? Will you start a pilgrim pathway to this celestial city?